BLOODY BR
HISTORy

WARWICK

BLOODY BRITISH HISTORY

HISTORY

WARWICK

GRAHAM SUTHERLAND

The
History
Press

First published in 2013
Reprinted in 2019

The History Press
97 St George's Place,
Cheltenham, Gloucestershire, GL50 3QB
www.thehistorypress.co.uk

ISBN 978 0 7524 9104 2

Typesetting and origination by The History Press
Printed in Great Britain by TJ International Ltd, Padstow, Cornwall

CONTENTS

AD 914

THE DANES ARE COMING

'Flee for your lives! The Danes are here!'

EARLY ONE MORNING in AD 791, the much-feared Danes arrived in Warwick and began to sack the settlement – then known as Wearwynk – yet again. During Warwick's history the settlement was sacked by raiders on at least four occasions – some historians say six times. Sadly, being raided by these fiendish warriors was an occupational hazard in pre-medieval England. Amongst Warwick's raiders were the Picts, Saxons and other barbarians. And this attack by the Danes was not to be their last incursion.

They came again in 1016.

When the raiders arrived, nobody was spared. The men would be slain and their women raped and carried off. Any child who survived would be carried off as well. Their livestock was either taken or slaughtered, along with anything else that could loosely be considered as having value. The raiders would leave a smoke-covered scene of havoc, slaughter and total desolation. Even local wildlife would shun the area for a while. The survivors would then be faced with the soul-destroying task of burying their dead and starting to rebuild their lives. Not all of them could cope with such tragedy; many left the area after an attack. But nowhere was safe from these raiders, especially the Danes.

However, that all started to change in 871 when Alfred the Great became king of Wessex: his military tactics meant that the Danes could no longer maraud wherever they wished in England. Alfred's eldest daughter, Ethelfleda, followed in her father's footsteps: although she was an educated woman, she became a very proficient soldier and formidable individual. In time she married Ethelred of Mercia, and the Danes had another formidable enemy to face.

A Pict. (THP)

7

THE MISSING CHILD

Ethelfleda had one child, a daughter who was called Elfwynne, who seems to have disappeared from history.

Having experienced the pangs of childbirth once, Ethelfleda had no intentions of ever having to go through them again. William of Malmesbury wrote: 'Who from the difficulty experienced in her first labour, ever after refused the embraces of her husband, protesting that it was unbecoming of the daughter of a king, to give way to a delight which after a time produced such consequence.'

Very little is known about Elfwynne's life, and even less about her death. It has been suggested she was deposed by Ethelfleda's brother, who succeeded her, but that may or not have been the case. She died in 919, the year after her mother.

Wessex consisted, roughly speaking, of Hampshire, Wiltshire, Dorset, Somerset and Berkshire. Mercia, on the other hand, covered what are mainly the Midlands today. An alliance, by marriage, between the two kingdoms made them a powerful force.

By now the Danes were colonising North-West England, but it did not stop them plundering other parts of the country. They were allowed to settle in Mercia, but it was an uneasy co-existence. Eventually Ethelred and Ethelfleda decided that enough was enough and declared war. Part of their tactics involved the construction of a series of fortifications, earth mounds topped by wooden palisades.

These were accompanied by new villages and towns (which would become known as boroughs). In time Ethelfleda came to Warwick where she built one such mound here in 914. With it she founded what was to become today's town.

Often known as the 'Lady of the Mercians', Ethelfleda was also described by the twelfth-century historian William of Malmesbury as being a 'spirited heroine'. Ethelfleda died in 918, having outlived her husband. She is buried in Gloucester Cathedral.

Although Warwick was only one of several new settlements Ethelfleda created, the town owes her a tremendous debt of gratitude.

AD 1068

CASTLE OF THE CONQUEROR

THE YEAR 1066 is probably the best-known date in English history. In this year, England was invaded by William the Conqueror – also referred to as William the Bastard, although never to his face. Ever-conscious of his illegitimacy, William was merciless towards anyone who reminded him of it: being blinded and/or having your hands cut off were amongst his more lenient punishments.

With such a reputation, Warwick's residents waited fearfully for the arrival of his representative to take over the small castle which had been founded in the previous century. In 1068, he arrived. Whilst it is popularly supposed that the 1st Earl of Warwick was created at the same time, this does not appear to have been the case; however, Henry de Newburgh was definitely the 1st Earl of Warwick by 1088. Henry won his title by remaining faithful to the new king, William II (known as 'Rufus', probably because of his red face), supporting him during a rebellion by the barons. The title Earl of Warwick was his reward.

The castle and its earls have played many important roles in the town's history, though not all of the earls lived

to tell the tale. Today the castle is a big tourist attraction, but in years gone by it was a place to be treated with respect and held in fear. The tools of torture can still be seen in the castle today. As lord of the manor the earl's word was law – or, in his absence, that of his deputies. He held the power of life or death over the miscreants who were brought before him. Trials were fair in name only and juries non-existent.

Suspected witches would have their hands tied to their feet before they were thrown into water: if they floated they were found guilty; their innocence would be proved if they sank. It did not matter to their accusers, who often included clergymen, if they drowned before they were brought to the surface. If a suspect had influential enemies the result could be fixed accordingly.

Other suspected criminals would undergo 'trial by ordeal'. Here the suspect was made to carry a lump of hot iron for three paces. The wound would be bound up and examined three days later. If the burn was healing, the defendant was thought to be innocent; if not, his or her guilt was thought proved, and suitable punishment – usually death or

mutilation – soon followed. There were of course a few loopholes: a suitable bribe could result in a cooler piece of iron to hold.

In theory torture was never legal in England – not that it made any real difference. If a confession was needed anything was considered acceptable: victims could be suspended from the ground by their wrists, and weights would sometimes be attached to their feet to make this even more painful. Normally it was sufficient for the unfortunate person just to hang, with his feet off the ground. Apart from the hideous swelling of his limbs, in a short period of time he would begin to suffer from all manner of chest pains.

Unlike its neighbour at Kenilworth, Warwick Castle was never really seriously besieged – there was a small event during the English Civil War, but that was all. With the invention and growing use of gunpowder the castle, along with most of its contemporaries, ceased to have a defensive role.

Suspension from the hands or feet, as illustrated in a book of 1591 (with a few horrible additions...). (THP)

Consequently, British castles were frequently converted into stately homes, usually at great expense.

Opposite *Warwick Castle then (Library of Congress, LC-DIG-ppmsc-08951) and now. (Author's collection)*

AD 1312

EVERY DOG HAS ITS DAY

The Horrible Death of Piers Gaveston!

Piers Gaveston awoke with a start when several heavily armed men invaded his bedroom. His heart sank. Amongst their stern faces was one he recognised and feared: it was Guy de Beauchamp, Earl of Warwick, whom he had nicknamed 'the Black Dog of Arden', and who was his most implacable enemy...

Piers Gaveston, 1st Earl of Cornwall (1284-1312) was the son of a fairly unimportant Gascon nobleman. He was described by a contemporary as 'graceful and agile in mind, sharp-witted, refined and well-versed in military matters'. However, other critics say this was just a façade, and that in reality he was 'arrogant, haughty, grasping and immature'. Growing up in Edward I's court, he and the young Prince Edward became long-standing friends – more than friends, in fact, if the rumours flying about the court were to be believed. (Today historians express some doubt concerning this suggestion. Both men had wives and had fathered children: were they more like brothers than lovers?)

Prince Edward's father, King Edward I, initially liked Gaveston, but by 1307 he had changed his mind. The king's temper was notorious. Edward I argued with his son about Gaveston and all the lavish gifts the prince had bestowed upon him, an argument which ended when Edward banished his son's favourite, after pulling out handfuls of his hair! Only too aware of Gaveston's malign influence, Edward knew he had to do something: on his deathbed, he instructed the Earls of Lincoln, Pembroke and Warwick to make sure that Gaveston's control over his son did not long continue. It might have been a very different story if they had succeeded...

When the prince became King Edward II in 1307, Gaveston's future was assured. He was soon exercising an increasing control over the new monarch – and they both succeeded in alienating the barons. The chorus of complaints eventually grew so loud that in February 1307 Edward was forced to temporarily exile his friend. As soon as he could, however, Edward II recalled him. He continued to reward his friend with all manner of gifts: horses, luxurious clothes and, on one occasion, £260 (approximately £128,000 today). He also gave him lands with

THE FOURTEENTH-CENTURY'S WORST BRITON

Hugh Despenser also met a grisly end, one which made Gaveston's death seem compara-tively easy and painless. Although he had opposed Gaveston's influence on the king, Despenser also became a royal favourite. Whilst it brought him tremendous power, for a while, like Gaveston he made many enemies among the barons. He was exiled in 1321, and turned to piracy for a while before returning to England (without permission). By 1326, Edward II was in a difficult position, being deserted on all sides by his supporters, and all because of his friendship with Despenser. It did not take long for Despenser to be tracked down, captured and tried as a traitor. The charge was returning from exile without permission. His conviction was a foregone conclusion, and the sentence of death by hanging, drawing and quartering was carried out immediately. One report states that – as he was castrated – he uttered a ghastly and inhuman howl just before he died.

an annual income in excess of £4,000 (approximately £1,950,000 today). Then, as a final mark of his love, Edward II made Gaveston Earl of Cornwall, a rank normally reserved for members of the royal family. His promotion joined the barons' growing list of grievances against Edward.

In 1308 Edward II went to France and married Philip IV's daughter. He appointed Gaveston to act as regent in his absence. Still secure in Edward's friendship, Gaveston made no effort to befriend the barons: instead, he continued to insult them. He called the Earl of Gloucester 'cuckold's bird' or 'whoreson'; he called Lancaster 'churl' or 'fiddler'; Lincoln 'burst-belly'; Pembroke 'Joseph the Jew'; and Warwick, because of his dark complexion, 'the Black Dog of Arden'.

It would prove to be a fatal mistake.

In 1311, when Edward returned, these powerful enemies forced his hand, and Gaveston was banished. Believing himself to be invincible, however, he once again returned. Not surprisingly, the earls of Hereford, Lancaster, Pembroke, Percy, Warren and Warwick lined up against the king, and civil war broke out. The king's supporters were pitifully few by comparison, with the main ones being Gloucester and Richmond.

Gaveston was eventually captured at Scarborough, and handed over to the Earl of Pembroke. Being an honourable man, the earl was tasked with escorting Gaveston to London – and he had every intention of doing so. However, on the way they stopped at Deddington. Believing Gaveston was safe, Pembroke went to visit his wife. But he had not reckoned on the 'Black Dog', who had other ideas.

A QUICK AND BLOODY END

Warwick, learning of Gaveston's whereabouts, quickly seized the prisoner. He was dragged to Warwick Castle for trial. A guilty verdict soon followed – and the sentence was death. In theory it was a legally valid trial and execution, but in reality it was a judicial murder.

Piers was unceremoniously escorted from the great hall, and in due course put on a horse, led through a hostile crowd in Warwick's streets, and on to the nearby Blacklow Hill (which was not on the Earl's land). All too soon, his last journey was over, and he was pulled from his horse. Two men were waiting with drawn swords. The first stabbed him in the chest, and the second removed his head in a swift fountain of blood. At long last the Earl of Warwick had taken his revenge. His arch enemy, Piers Gaveston, Earl of Cornwall, was dead.

The monument erected at the site reads:

In the hollow of this Rock
Was beheaded
On the 1st day of July 1312
By Barons as lawless as himself
PIERS GAVESTON Earl of Cornwall
The minion of a hateful king
In Life and Death
A Memorable Instance of Misrule

After his headless body had fallen to the ground, the entire party moved off, leaving Gaveston where he had fallen in the woods on Blacklow Hill. No one was told what to do with his corpse.

Some time later four shoemakers came from Warwick and took Gaveston back to the town. However, no one in the town would accept his body. Finally, therefore, his body was removed to Oxford (which was where Pembroke had appealed for

The head of Piers Gaveston. (THP)

Gaveston's release to his custody). The city was quite prepared to accept the body, but there was a major problem: Gaveston had been excommunicated, which meant that he could not be buried in consecrated ground.

Edward II was beside himself with rage when he heard what had happened. He kept Gaveston's embalmed body with him wherever he went. In due course the excommunication order was rescinded, but Edward remained unwilling to release his friend's body. Finally it was forcibly removed from him and buried in the Dominican Priory at Kings Langley, Hertfordshire.

Gaveston's Memorial. (Author's collection)

DEATH TO WOMEN AND KINGS

Two of Warwick's Deadliest Earls Revealed!

RICHARD BEAUCHAMP (1381-1439), 13TH EARL OF WARWICK

'Be of good heart: it is done. She is caught this time.' With these words, Pierre Cauchon, Bishop of Beauvais, sealed the fate of Joan of Arc. They would also embroil Richard Beauchamp (1381-1439) in controversy for centuries to come.

Richard Beauchamp was the 13th Earl of Warwick. He was knighted in 1401, at the coronation of Henry IV, and by then he was already proving himself to be a capable soldier, administrator, and a good friend to Henry V.

Soon afterwards he was sent to fight in Wales against Owain Glyndwr. During his early campaigns he acquired a reputation for chivalry, taking part in many sporting combats – he was even the queen's champion at one stage. Nonetheless his power and loyalty grew, and he remained totally devoted to his king. This explains why he was entrusted with the young Henry VI's education and welfare.

In 1429 the English faced a new and formidable enemy in the unlikely form of a seventeen-year-old French girl known as Joan of Arc, who dressed in male clothing (cross-dressing being a capital offence at the time, as it was regarded as being against natural law). In a surprising turn of fortune, she persuaded King Charles VII of France to give her command of the French army. It has never been fully understood why he did so. In a superstitious world, her enemies were quick to maintain she had bewitched him. Whatever the reason, giving her overall command led to a massive uplift in the French fortunes: after only a few weeks she had succeeded where all others had failed, leading her troops from one victory to the next. The English were on the run.

Richard Beauchamp travelled to France with a huge army and managed, by a stroke of luck, to capture Joan. Initially she was moved from one prison to another whilst her captors negotiated her sale to the highest bidder. With such a formidable reputation, there was no real chance of her being returned to the French. Finally she was purchased by Beauchamp and Pierre Cauchon, in whose diocese she had been captured. Joan was taken to Rouen, where Cauchon had her tried for heresy and

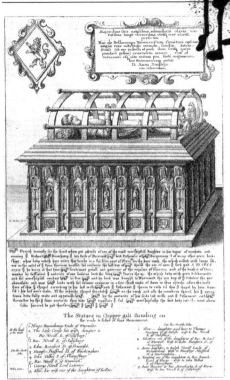

Capture of Joan of Arc. (THP)

Tomb of Richard Beauchamp, the 13th Earl of Warwick. (With kind permission of the Thomas Fisher Rare Book Library, Univeristy of Toronto)

cross from two pieces of wood and gave it to her. Then the fire was lit. Traditionally, the executioner climbed up to his victims and strangled them before the fire got too hot. But he was not able to do so in Joan's case: she died slowly, writhing in agony before the flames destroyed her body, whilst the smell of her burning flesh filled the air. A flock of doves flew away from the castle as she died. Twenty-five years later the Pope pronounced her innocence, and in 1909 she was declared a martyr and beatified.

The English king at the time was only nine years old, and many have suggested that Joan was mistreated, and indeed executed, at the suggestion of the Earl of Warwick.

witchcraft. As far as the English were concerned, she was a witch.

It was not an easy imprisonment for Joan, as she was regularly subjected to sexual abuse, eventually forcing the earl to change her guards.

She was tried and sentenced to life imprisonment in February 1431. Four days later Joan was found wearing men's clothing, which had been conveniently left in her cell; her own had been removed. She was now found guilty of heresy and sentenced to death. On 30 May she was taken to the old market place in Rouen and tied to a stake, surrounded by faggots of wood. A kindly disposed English soldier fashioned a

RICHARD NEVILLE (1428-1471), 16TH EARL OF WARWICK

One of the most famous Earls of Warwick is Richard Neville (1428-1471), 16th Earl of Warwick, remembered by history as 'the Kingmaker'.

Described as being one of the most powerful and wealthiest of men, Richard

17

THE HISTORY OF CROSS-DRESSING

Over the centuries many women have worn male clothing, illegal or not. For women who served in the army or navy this was one way of hiding their gender; it was also more practical to wear. However, cross-dressing was not restricted to females: in the age when press gangs forcibly abducted men into the navy, likely recruits adopted all manner of ruses to avoid capture. One was to wear women's clothing, although the press gangs were well aware of such tricks.

In south and west Wales, male participants in the Rebecca Riots wore female clothing as a disguise. These riots happened in 1839 and 1840 in protest against various taxes – not just against tollgates, for attacks on which they are mainly remembered.

Neville lived up to his nickname. During his life he helped crown two kings: Henry VI and Edward IV. He was a very capable and efficient soldier, blessed with a charisma which appealed to his followers. The governor of Abbeville once wrote a letter to Louis XI in which he discussed the situation in England. 'They have but two rulers: Monsieur de Warwick and another whose name I have forgotten.'

Richard Neville. (THP)

The period known as the Wars of the Roses lasted from 1455 to 1485, during which there were numerous battles of varying sizes. Possibly one of the most memorable was Towton, in 1461. Often referred to as the largest and bloodiest battle ever fought on English soil, it saw 50,000 men fight during a snowstorm on Palm Sunday. When the battle was over, 28,000 men lay dead – both sides having decided not to take prisoners. In one of his characteristically charismatic gestures, it is said that Neville killed his horse just before the battle began so he would not be tempted to ride away from the conflict. 'Let him fly that will, for surely I will tarry with him that will tarry with me,' he reportedly said.

Then Neville fell out with the king, a conflict which ended bloodily at the Battle of Barnet in April 1471. Here he made another gesture regarding his horse – but in this case it backfired. During Easter Saturday night Warwick ordered his artillery to fire on Edward's camp. For the remainder of the night his cannons fired salvo after salvo, but to no avail: unbeknownst to Warwick's commanders, Edward

do so on foot. His plate armour was very heavy, restricted his movements, and was tiring. Regardless of the weather, it was always very hot inside the armour.

Warwick discovered he had been fooled when Edward made a surprise attack. Just then, Warwick received some much-needed reinforcements – but in the mist they were mistaken for more of Edward's men. Believing they were being attacked, Warwick's men turned on the advancing soldiers. By the time the mistake was realised, all was lost for Warwick. He fled the field, having already seen his brother killed. Slowed down by his armour, he was attacked from behind and knocked over. Lying helpless on the ground, he was unable to stop his enemies lifting up his visor and stabbing him to death.

Warwick killing his horse at the Battle of Towton. (THP)

had taken advantage of the heavy mist which had risen and moved his troops. During the night, as the mist thickened, Warwick's force's morale suffered – not that it had ever been very high. After many years of Civil War, most of the soldiers were tired of fighting. The heavy mist added to their misery, making everything damp and cold. They just wanted to go home.

As day broke, they took up their formation unenthusiastically and waited.

Well aware of their low morale, Warwick's commanders agreed to fight on foot. This decision was meant to show their soldiers that they would not abandon the battlefield at a moment's notice. It was not an easy task for a knight, dressed to fight from a horse, to

Death of the Earl of Warwick at the Battle of Barnet. (THP)

HAVE A DRINK ON ME

Following the Kingmaker's death, his title went to his son-in-law. His name was George Plantagenet, 1st Duke of Clarence. Although he inherited the title, he did not inherit most of the estate.

George married Warwick's eldest daughter, Isabel Neville, in 1469, and always felt a misplaced loyalty to his father-in-law in his struggles against Edward IV (George's brother). Sometime after his father-in-law's death George took part in a plot against Edward which was discovered. He was arrested, found guilty of treason, and sentenced to be privately executed. And this is where the mystery really begins, as no one knows what happened to him next... Some time ago, a skeleton was found buried in the Tower of London, and was supposed to be his. George, it was believed, had been beheaded – but there were no such injuries on this skeleton. If this was indeed George's skeleton, what had killed the Duke of Clarence? In his play *Richard III*, William Shakespeare came up with an ingenious solution: George Plantagenet is known as 'false, fleeting perjured Clarence', and is drowned in a butt of Malmsey wine. (A butt would have held 105 gallons, which would have been more than enough to drown him in.)

Another Warwick connection exists between the duke and the town. When George's wife Isabel died, he became convinced that she had been poisoned by one of her ladies-in-waiting, a woman by the name of Ankarette Twynyho. The *Calendar of the Patent Rolls Preserved in the Public Office* describes what happened next:

Richard Hyde late of Warwick, gentleman, and Roger Strugge late of Bekehampton, co. Somerset, towker, with divers riotous persons to the number of fourscore by the command of George, duke of Clarence, came ... about two of the clock afternoon and entered her [Ankarette's] house and carried her ... to Warwick ... and then and there took from her all her jewels, money and goods.

...The said duke kept Ankarette in prison unto the hour of nine before noon on the morrow ... and then caused her to be brought to the Guildhall at Warwick before divers of the justices of the peace in the county then sitting in sessions and caused her to be indicted by the name of Ankarette Twynneowe, late of Warwick, widow, late servant of the duke and Isabel his wife, of having at Warwick on 10 October, 16 Edward IV., given to the said Isabel a venomous drink of ale mixed with poison, of which the latter sickened until the Sunday before Christmas, on which day she died, and the justices arraigned the said Ankarette and a jury appeared and found her guilty and it was considered that she should be led from the bar there to the gaol of Warwick and from thence should be drawn through the town to the gallows of Myton and hanged till she were dead, and the sheriff was commanded to do execution and so he did.

To prove the brothers were dead, Edward had their bodies stripped and displayed at St Paul's Cathedral for three days before allowing them to be buried.

Bosworth, in 1485, brought the Wars of the Roses to a close – but not before Richard III had been killed. His body has, of course, just been discovered underneath a Leicester car park.

THE MAN WHO MIGHT HAVE BEEN KING

TO SAY THAT Robert Dudley, 1st Earl of Leicester (sometimes spelt Leycester) was far from happy as he rode into Warwick in 1571 is an understatement. He was accompanied by a large party of friends, and was furious to find that there was no welcoming party to greet him. This was not the way a favourite and friend of Queen Elizabeth I – and the man who at one point looked to be a likely husband for her – expected to be treated.

It eventually transpired that there had been a misunderstanding over the dates: the welcome had been planned for the following day.

Dudley's early life had not been without its problems. He was the fifth son of John Dudley, 1st Duke of Northumberland and Earl of Warwick. His brother John Guildford Dudley had been married to Lady Jane Grey, who had ruled as queen for nine days. The unfortunate Jane is remembered for having the shortest reign in English history. His father and brother were executed when that lady fell. Robert Dudley, who had been caught up in the events, was arrested and sentenced to death. Luckily for him this sentence was never carried out, and he was released to take up a military career.

In the course of his life, Dudley was sympathetic to Mary Queen of Scots. However, he refused to marry her. He enjoyed the reputation of being a competent sportsman, excelling at tennis (not the lawn variety), and he regularly partnered Elizabeth at dances. Unusually for his time, he did not enjoy the rich food served up at banquets and when he had the choice always preferred to eat exotic fruits and salads. Described as being the 'goodliest male personage' in England, he was skilled in languages and composition. Unfortunately, Dudley became involved in a war with Holland which was a military and a financial disaster. Back home he regularly backed Sir Francis Drake and others in their ventures. In 1588 he had overall command of the English land forces at the time of the Armada, and was responsible for Elizabeth I reviewing her troops at Tilbury.

Dudley had come to complete the arrangements for the funding of a hospital, which would provide accommodation for twelve veteran soldiers. He had settled on adapting the old Guildhall (now part of the Lord Leycester Hospital) for this purpose. Seriously offended by the lack of a welcoming party, Dudley considered changing his mind, and having the hospital built at Kenilworth. Whilst this idea appealed to the about-to-be-displaced-from-the-Guildhall schoolmaster, the town's officials were not so happy. It would be a disastrous mistake to offend Elizabeth's favourite. Once it was realised what had happened, a delegation, complete with two oxen as a peace offering, went to the priory where Dudley was staying. In no mood for discussion, he ignored them for the next thirty-six hours; he then returned to Kenilworth. When he finally condescended to see them his temper had not improved. Slowly, however, he relented, and agreed the hospital should be in Warwick, where it still stands today.

It is not a hospital in the medical sense, but provides accommodation for retired personnel from the Armed Services. The hospital was finally up and running, after being granted its own charter in 1571 by Elizabeth I. Strict rules governed the way the residents behaved, including:

- Heresy, adultery, drunkenness, blasphemy, larceny, quarrelling and fornication were banned
- No hounds or hawks to be kept in the rooms
- Brothel visiting and gaming were not allowed
- Church attendance compulsory
- Nights out not allowed without permission
- Uniform to be worn in town
- No female servants allowed under the age of sixty
- Marriage only permitted with special permission
- No begging, damaging hedges or stealing firewood allowed

Above *Robert Dudley's tomb.*

Left *Robert Dudley's tomb, as it was then. (With kind permission of the Thomas Fisher Rare Book Library, University of Toronto)*

DEATH AT CUMNOR PLACE

In 1560, Amy Robsart, the wife of Robert Dudley, died in mysterious circumstances at Cumnor Place (rather than at Kenilworth, as is often erroneously suggested).

It cannot have been easy for Amy, daughter of a wealthy Norfolk gentleman, to play second fiddle to the queen. As he was Elizabeth's master of horse, which was a very important position, Dudley spent much of his time at court. Whatever his marital ambitions towards the queen might have been, they certainly could not happen if he was a divorcee. Only as a widower could Dudley marry Elizabeth.

On the day of her death Amy had stayed alone at home whilst the servants had gone to a nearby fair. When they returned they found her body at the foot of her stairs. Once the gossips started whispering, Elizabeth had no choice but to order an enquiry into Amy's death, and banish Dudley from court (albeit temporarily). Whilst

Elizabeth I. (Library of Congress, LC-USZ62-47605)

the enquiry absolved Dudley from any wrongdoing (could it have done anything else?), the question still remains today: did she fall or was she pushed? Whatever the answer, the death left a cloud hanging over Dudley. This meant that he could never marry Elizabeth, although they remained firm friends.

Then, in March 1578, he secretly married Lettice Knollys, widow of the 1st Earl of Essex. When Elizabeth heard of it she was furious, and banished her permanently from court. To make matters worse for the couple, she kept Dudley away from his wife as much as she possibly could. Then rumours began to spread that Dudley had murdered Lettice's husband, the Earl of Essex, so that he could marry her. Essex reportedly died of dysentery but claimed that he had been poisoned. Dudley was the number one suspect. It is unlikely that he was responsible, but his enemies still voiced the allegations.

With such a track record there was no way Elizabeth could marry him. However, she was beside herself with grief when he died in 1588. She kept all his letters, until her dying day, in her box of treasures.

Lettice had Dudley buried in the Beauchamp Chapel at St Mary's church. Although he left her well provided for, Dudley also had a considerable number of debts (many of which were due to Elizabeth, who lost no time in claiming them from his hated widow).

Another one of Dudley's chickens came home to roost when an illegitimate son, also called Robert Dudley, tried to claim the estate from Lettice. He maintained that he was the product of an earlier legitimate marriage; the courts, however, found in the widow's favour. When Lettice died in 1634, at the age of ninety-one, she was buried alongside her husband. It is interesting to note that the effigy on her side of the tomb is higher than his!

Lord Leycester Hospital. (Author's collection)

Only within the last century have the brethren been allowed to have their own individual accommodation. Prior to that, and still within some people's memories, they shared the Guildhall and lived in curtained-off spaces, with little or no privacy. Today they enjoy proper accommodation.

In the same year Dudley attended St Mary's church, Warwick, where he celebrated being invested with the Order of St Michael which had been previously awarded to him by Charles IX of France. Back in Warwick, he was escorted by the bailiff and the town's burgesses to St Mary's church – but nothing could have prepared the watchers for how Dudley was dressed. With the exception of his hat, which was black, he was dressed in white and silver. Twice during the service he placed gold pieces in the alms plate on the altar. Afterwards he returned to the priory, where he dined alone.

QUEEN ELIZABETH'S VISIT TO WARWICK

Queen Elizabeth I visited Warwick in August 1572, when she was entertained by a firework display in the evening.

The display was meant to represent a mock attack on two wooden forts which had been specially erected for the purpose. Unfortunately, the attack was too realistic and a fireball landed on the roof of a nearby cottage in Bridge End. Fire quickly spread to the two adjoining buildings, which also burnt down, injuring two elderly people.

Her Majesty sent them £25 (approximately £4,700 today) to help with their repairs. It is not known if she sent money to all the victims.

Great Seal of Elizabeth I. (THP)

AD 1570

SCANDALOUS SCENES AS LOCAL BENEFACTOR DIES

'If Mr Oken did ever speak again the town should have not one groat of his goods, nor land, neither if they could help it!' cried one of Thomas Oken's executors to the others.

Suddenly the truth was out.

They would gain very little, if anything at all, following the death of the richest man in Warwick. This was not what they had expected, and certainly not what they had wanted...

Warwick man Thomas Oken had a wife, Joan, who had predeceased him. Having no children, he willed much of his considerable fortune for the benefit of Warwick. It was a move that was guaranteed to be unpopular with some people – especially his executors. To complicate matters, Thomas had actually made two wills, both on the same day, in 1570.

At first glance they appeared to be identical, but a closer inspection revealed significant differences between them. The first one did not contain any bequests for the town, with his money going just to his friends, particularly the executors of his will. It was the second will which caused all the grief. This one instructed that all of his money, with the exception of a few bequests, went for the benefit of the town.

As long as Thomas lived, there was no problem – but unfortunately Thomas was dying, and his death would open a large can of worms. There was no way the executors would approve of all his wealth going to the town. It remains a mystery why he left two wills: being the astute businessman that he was, he must have foreseen that problems would arise.

Thomas was a far-seeing man. He had to have been in order to survive. Apart from acknowledging Lady Jane Grey's abortive time on the throne of England, he was a staunch Roman Catholic, which was not always the safest religion to practice. Nevertheless, he helped to

Oken's house. (Author's Collection)

steer Warwick through the difficult times of the Reformation.

Possibly he had anticipated difficulties with the second will: he named an additional half-a-dozen worthy townsmen to act as overseers and ensure that the executors complied with the terms.

As Thomas had appointed the same executors for both wills, they knew only too well just how much money they stood to lose. They therefore began to plan their response should the second will be upheld. Several hours before Thomas died he was visited by a local clergyman and by one of the overseers of the second will. They confirmed that the second will – i.e. the one which gave money to the town – was the one Oken favoured. The executors were far from happy at this news, and made no secret of their views to overseer Thomas Powell. He went to the town clerk (another overseer) and

told him about what had happened. He also shared his suspicions about the executors. Soon afterwards, all the overseers went to Oken's house, wanting to see him again.

But by now he could no longer speak.

This worried the executors, who were also in the house. The overseers demanded to examine both wills. When they went to remove the second all-important will there was a scuffle: the executors tried to seize it, and part of it was damaged. The overseers refused to give way, and finally left the house – taking the will with them for safe keeping.

Later, two of the executors' wives returned to Oken's room, where he lay in a coma. Even if he knew what was happening, he was powerless to do anything about it.

Not content with just shouting, they tried to wake him up and change

ARRESTING WILLIAM SHAKESPEARE

The first Lucys came to England with William the Conqueror, and by 1247 they were established in Charlecote Park, not far from Warwick. Although resembling a sixteenth-century building, complete with a deer park and Capability Brown-influenced gardens, most of the house is in fact Victorian. Today the house is owned by the National Trust.

Sir Thomas Lucy, who was the arbiter in this settlement of Oken's will, was a Member of Parliament, and had been responsible for catching Shakespeare poaching deer and rabbits on his land – or so the folklore goes. But this was not the only run-in he had with Shakespeare's family. Being an ardent Protestant, and a magistrate, he was responsible for catching and interrogating Roman Catholics. Whilst Shakespeare was not a Catholic, various members of his mother's Arden family were. Undoubtedly they would have been on his hit list. One of them, Edward Arden, was William's mother's second cousin. He was implicated in a plot to assassinate Queen Elizabeth I. Sir Thomas Lucy was responsible for his arrest, and the man was later hanged at Tyburn. It has been suggested that he actually knew nothing about the plot but had been maliciously implicated by Robert Dudley...

In later life Shakespeare lampooned Sir Thomas as Mr Justice Shallow in the *Merry Wives of Windsor* and *Henry VI, Part 2*.

his mind about the will. But it was to no avail, and only resulted in crowds gathering outside the house.

LOCKED DOORS AND ABUSE

On the next day Thomas Oken died, and the struggle over the wills began. From the very start the executors made matters as difficult as they could. Once they realised that Oken was dead, they locked themselves in one of his rooms and began dividing up the spoils. Oken's housekeeper saw them and she tried to stop it: when they ignored her, she went straight to the overseers and reported what was happening.

Sir Thomas Lucy hearing the case.

They quickly went to Oken's house, only to be met with locked doors and abuse. Whilst the overseers could not get into the house, they made sure the executors could not get out of it. It was a stand-off.

Common sense finally took over, and the executors opened the doors. A great deal of haggling followed before the overseers left the house sometime after midnight.

Very unwillingly, the executors agreed to have the second will proved and pay the legacies. But there was a big difference between what they agreed to do and what they actually did. The agreed deadline of Michaelmas came and passed, and the beneficiaries demanded to know when they would be paid. Their demands were ignored, and by Easter 1574 the matter still had not been resolved. The executors were in no hurry and were as obstructive as possible – they still wanted the first will to be proved.

Finally, Sir Thomas Lucy from nearby Charlecote – the man who had caught William Shakespeare poaching – was appointed as arbiter. After hearing both sides, he agreed the overseers had acted correctly and ordered the executors to pay the legacies. They agreed to do so, but only when the overseers stopped harassing them!

They were determined to have the last word.

AD 1604

TRAITORS OR MARTYRS?

The Executions of Father John Sugar and Robert Grissold

BY 1604 ENGLAND had been a Protestant country for over fifty years. When Elizabeth became queen in 1553 the papacy could have ended the friction between the two religions, but instead it chose to declare open season on her. The Pope even offered papal dispensation for anyone who assassinated the 'Whore of Babylon', as Elizabeth was known to many Roman Catholics. Elizabeth's ministers retaliated, and began a full-scale persecution of Roman Catholics which continued after her death.

Although banned, many Catholics still secretly followed their faith. Some of them hatched plots against Elizabeth, and later James I, none of which succeeded. Many were encouraged by Father John Sugar's fellow Jesuit priests.

Father John Sugar was born in 1558 at Wombourn in Staffordshire, and was educated at Oriel College, Oxford, although he never graduated. Later on he was ordained at Douai, and sent on his fatal mission to Rowington. Very little is known about Robert Grissold other than he came from Rowington and was employed by Mr Sheldon in nearby Broadway.

Recent research absolves Father John of being involved in any such plots, and confirms that he was only interested in the religious welfare of his fellow Catholics. But all Jesuits were banned from England, and they faced the death penalty if they were caught. Jesuits had large prices on their heads, and many of them, including Father John, were betrayed. As their main aim was to support the Catholic faith, which was outlawed in England, they were classed as traitors – and dealt with accordingly.

For English Jesuits it was a difficult choice: their country or their faith? Would they be traitors or martyrs? In reality it made little difference, as the penalty was the same: execution in a very unpleasant manner.

A DREADFUL END

Father John and his servant had been arrested at Rowington the previous year, and kept in gaol since then. There had been a reluctance to put them on trial, but ultimately the authorities were forced to act. After being sentenced to death, the pair spent their last night

DID THE JESUITS SINK THE *TITANIC?*

Although founded in the sixteenth century, the Society of Jesus remains an active Roman Catholic organisation. Over the years its members, called Jesuits, have made countless enemies both within their own faith and elsewhere. They have also been the victims of several plots.

One far-fetched conspiracy theory blames them for the sinking of the *Titanic* in 1912. The alleged plot involved some Jesuit American bankers who wanted to set up a central bank (now called the Federal Reserve), with the active backing of their government. As expected, there was some opposition to the proposal. These opponents had to be eliminated, preferably in a spectacular fashion (to act as a warning to others). The plan was to fund the building of the *Titanic*, ensure that their opponents were on-board and then send them down with the ship. That part of the scheme involved Captain Smith, allegedly a Jesuit brother. He was instructed, according to the theory, to sail the *Titanic* at full speed, on a moonless night, through a conveniently placed ice-field; to ignore all the warnings he had been given; and to go down with his ship. Any innocent parties who were killed were to be counted as collateral damage.

Several months after the *Titanic* sank, all opposition to the Federal Reserve stopped. It has been suggested that the warning of the *Titanic* had been received!

Titanic *sinking. (THP)*

praying, but all too soon their cell door was opened by armed guards.

Slowly the procession moved off towards the appropriately named Gallows Hill at nearby Heathcote, accompanied by hundreds of spectators. Some of them were inevitably in favour of the executions, but many others were silently praying. As a convicted traitor, Father John was dragged to the execution site on a wooden hurdle, symbolically showing him to be the lowest form of life. Condemned men were originally dragged to their executions along the ground, which often caused their deaths before the executioner could get at them. Hurdles lessened the chances of that happening.

Robert Grissold's only crime had been to serve his master. Since his trial Grissold had refused to save his life by renouncing his Catholic faith. He walked through the mud at Father John's side as they went to their deaths.

The executioner was waiting for them with a fire already burning, and his knives and axe sharpened. As the ghoulish crowd watched, he began his dreadful task. First, Father John was hanged. Then, still breathing, he was cut down and stripped. He was castrated, and his belly cut open. His internal organs were then pulled out and thrown into the fire as he watched. Finally the axe was raised, and his head was cut off. Stooping down, the executioner picked it up, still dripping blood, and showed it to the crowd, shouting, 'Behold the head of a traitor!' Then, using the same bloody axe, the executioner cut the body into four quarters, ready to be spiked upon the town gates.

Grissold watched all of this, even moving a woman who tried to shield him from the sight to one side, telling her, 'Stand away, for I thank God that the sight doth nothing terrify me.' He told the executioner, as he came for him, 'You do me wrong, in keeping me alive so long after Mr Sugar, for I should have suffered with him, and I only desire to be with him.' Grissold then picked up the rope with which he was to be hanged and dipped it in his friend's blood. He then climbed up the ladder. 'I die for my conscience,' he told the crowd. Moments later he was pulled off his feet and strangled, though as a small mercy he was left hanging until he was quite dead.

Both men were beatified in 1987.

AD 1605

REMEMBER! REMEMBER!

Terrorists Strike in Warwick

'**F**AWKES IS TAKEN!'
These were the last words Robert Catesby (*c.*1572-1605) wished to hear. They meant that his gang had failed to blow up Parliament and the Protestant king to restore Roman Catholicism to England. All their meticulous planning had been wasted.

James I would still be alive at the end of the day.

Although Catesby did not have a specific fall-back plan, he was convinced they could still succeed – but he had to act swiftly. Guy Fawkes could not hold out indefinitely under torture. No one did. After the gentler methods failed to produce results, he would be put on the rack.

And that never failed to loosen tongues.

Strictly speaking, torture was only justified in exceptional circumstances, but Catesby knew Fawkes fell easily into this category. Already he could see the unfortunate man hanging by his wrists, and having heavy weights attached to his feet ... and that was only the beginning.

THE GATHERING AT DUNCHURCH

Abandoning the plan of stopping at his mother's house in Ashby-St-Ledgers, he rode on. (She heard his horse galloping by, realised things had gone wrong, and knew she might never see her son again.) Catesby did not stop until he had reached Dunchurch, near Rugby, where most of his fellow conspirators were waiting for him, accompanied by a large group of young men (all Roman Catholics) who thought they had been invited to take part in a hunting party.

They had no idea that Catesby intended them to spearhead a rebellion in Warwickshire.

Once Catesby had told them the real reason they were there they quickly left him and fled back home: they wanted nothing to do with such a hare-brained scheme. Catesby was left with only his original supporters and a couple of new recruits. In spite of having failed to blow up Parliament, he still believed their plot could succeed and his next move was towards Warwick. Initially his men believed they would bypass the town and go to nearby Norbrook

31

The conspirators at work in the vault. (THP)

Arrest of Guy Fawkes. (THP)

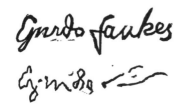

His signature before and after torture. (THP)

Grange, where conspirator John Grant lived. Grant also believed this was where they were heading: to collect the arms, ammunition and horses that he had amassed for them. But Catesby had other ideas.

NOT WANTED

Grant's horses were of a smaller breed, and they did not have the stamina of coursers (which were specially bred war horses). These animals would be vital for his ever-depleting band of men. Catesby knew there were coursers at Warwick Castle, which was where he was now headed. His plan was not popular. It received many unfavourable responses, but objections were to no avail: once Catesby had made up his mind, no amount of reasoning would make him change it. He was also a master swordsman, and not someone to upset. With such a fearsome reputation, he forced through his plan to steal horses from Warwick Castle. Reluctantly the conspirators complied with his instructions (although they were convinced it was a big mistake).

Shortly before midnight, the gang stole as many of the coursers as they could handle. Leaving Warwick, they went to Norbrook Grange, stopping only long enough to collect Grant's arms and ammunition.

But now Catesby was in for an unpleasant surprise, as his hopes of support from the local Roman Catholics did not materialise. They had more sense. Doors were shut against Catesby and his men: they were most definitely not welcome. It was obvious

UNLUCKY THIRTEEN

The Gunpowder Plot had many Warwickshire connections. Its figurehead, Robert Catesby, was born in Lapworth, not far from Warwick. Guy Fawkes is the most infamous member of the plot, and is sometimes looked upon as 'the fall guy' in this sorry affair. But do not have any sympathy for Fawkes. He was the only one with experience of gunpowder, and if he had succeeded in blowing up the Houses of Parliament the death toll would have been horrendous. In recent times historians have begun to question the roles of each of the plotters. Was the plan really organised by Catesby, or had it in fact been masterminded by Robert Cecil, the king's devious chief minister and spymaster, as a way of discrediting Roman Catholics?

Regardless of whose idea it was, the Gunpowder Plot certainly set back the Roman Catholic cause in England for many years. In total there were thirteen original plotters – not an auspicious number!

to all that their great enterprise was now a dismal failure.

Once the theft of the coursers had been discovered, a hue and cry soon started after them. The trail of a large party of men, riding good-quality horses, was easy to follow.

HOLBEACH HOUSE

Ragged and terrified, the group finally arrived at Holbeach House, on the Worcestershire and Staffordshire borders, where they made a last stand. They had already lost one conspirator: during the night the men had decided to dry their wet gunpowder in front of an open fire. It exploded, blinding John Grant. Next day, Friday 8 November, the sheriff of Worcester and his troops arrived. Catesby was killed with the

Catesby slain. (Author's collection)

first shot, and three other conspirators quickly followed. The others were ultimately hanged, drawn and quartered.

We shall never know how quickly they would have been caught if they had not stolen those coursers from Warwick Castle.

33

THE CIVIL WAR IN WARWICK

WHEN CHARLES I succeeded to the throne in 1625, no one could possibly have foreseen just how his reign would end. In fact, had his elder brother Henry not died in 1612 this part of English history could have been very different.

Initially it was hoped that Charles would continue with his father's strong Protestant foreign policy against Roman Catholic countries, but this was not to be. Matters were not helped when he married the French princess Henrietta Maria, also in 1625: she was a Roman Catholic.

Charles was a firm believer in the Divine Right of Kings, which stipulated that the king was God's representative on Earth, and he could do no wrong. Sadly, it was an outmoded principle which soon brought him into conflict with Parliament. Matters went from bad to worse, culminating in his ill-judged action in entering Parliament, at the head of his troops, intent on arresting five members (all of whom had already left). He had accused them of treason, but entering Parliament in such a manner was a gross abuse of his royal prerogative.

For many parliamentarians, it was the final straw.

Matters went from bad to worse, and civil war became inevitable. After several skirmishes, the first real battle took place on 23 October 1642 at Edgehill, situated between Warwick and Banbury. The result was inconclusive, and the Midlands became the scene of several other battles before the final one, at Naseby in 1645, in which the Royalist cause was defeated.

Whilst there were several battles in this war, most of them were not on the same scale as Edgehill, Marston Moor (1644) and Naseby. They tended to be much smaller engagements, often in and around fortified houses and castles. Once such engagement took place at Warwick Castle in August 1642.

CASTLE UNDER ATTACK

Robert Greville, 2nd Baron Brooke of Warwick, was a strong parliamentarian supporter. Consequently, so was the town of Warwick, as it followed his views. In reality it did not make too much difference to the local inhabitants which side they supported: if they were pro-Parliament then they were expected to provide food and supplies for that army; at the same time, if there were Royalist troops in the town then they had to provide *them* with food and supplies! It was the same for Royalist supporters.

In late July 1642 Greville was confronted by Spencer Compton, Warwickshire's lord lieutenant and an ardent Royalist. Greville had been transporting several pieces of artillery to Warwick, but following Compton's intervention he was obliged to leave them at Banbury. On 7 August Compton appeared, with the captured cannons, and laid siege to Warwick Castle.

William Dugdale, dressed in the red and gold finery of the Croix Rouge Pursuivant (which identified him as a junior officer of arms of the College of Heraldry), demanded the castle's surrender. His demands were refused.

As sieges went it was not a particularly important one. It seemed as if neither side knew what to do next. In fact, Charles I had not yet raised his standard. At some stage one of the Royalist besiegers had an idea: 'If you mount your cannons up in Saint Mary's church, then you'll be able to fire down into the castle.'

This simple and obvious idea was not greeted with any great deal of enthusiasm by the men who had to carry the cannons up to the top of the tower. But orders were orders, and in due course all was ready for the great enterprise. The cannons were in position, loaded – and fired. After the smoke had cleared the gunners peered expectantly towards the castle to see what damage they had done. Not a lot! All of their hard

William Dugdale. (With kind permission of the Thomas Fisher Rare Book Library, University of Toronto)

work had been for nothing. In the words of one of the Royalists, 'Our endeavours for taking it were to little purpose.'

Very few reports of the siege have survived. One agrees that the Royalists did little damage. It was then the turn of the defenders to fight back. They fired into the streets and killed several Royalist troops. Their artillery then turned on the church and brought down one of the pinnacles onto the Royalists – who quickly abandoned the idea of firing from the church. A local Royalist-supporting butcher paraded in front of the castle, carrying a shoulder of lamb and taunting the defenders. He cannot have been surprised when one of the defenders shot him dead. In another exchange of shots, a resident in West Street had his house damaged by fire from the castle. He later submitted a claim for £4 damages (approximately

£360 today). It is not recorded if this claim was ever paid.

The siege ended on 23 August, which was the day after Charles I raised his standard in Nottingham, to encourage men to join his growing army. It was a very windy day, and his standard was blown over, which was considered to be an unlucky omen – borne out by his army's eventual defeat. His original plan had been to raise his standard in Warwickshire and capture Warwick Castle, hoping this action would have ended the war before it even began. But he was too late.

The castle was not attacked again, although it was used to hold Royalist prisoners. For the remainder of the war Warwick went about as normal, and took little or no real further part in the conflict.

LIFE IN WARWICK

With the abandonment of the siege, Greville set about improving the castle's defences and made it almost impregnable, thereby preventing Charles from trying to capture it again. However, such improvements resulted in some town houses being demolished and gardens destroyed.

As is the way, the war led to some people making money whilst others lost it. Suddenly there was a great demand for food, clothes, leather boots, harnesses, et cetera. In the immediate post-Edgehill period, apothecaries made plenty of money supplying medicines and bandages to the castle (where many of the wounded soldiers had been taken). On the negative side, trade at the markets declined dramatically. The local troops were also quite happy to plunder shops and houses at will – regardless of the fact that their owners were on the same side. Ultimately, however, they realised that these actions were counter-productive. The castle's commander, John Bridges, operated a policy which was nothing short of highway robbery: his men, under the excuse of 'looking for Royalist supplies', either plundered local travellers or else charged them a fee to be left alone.

As the war progressed Warwick became an important parliamentarian centre with an almost impregnable castle. However, there were occasions when its garrison was required elsewhere. When that happened, local men were pressed into garrison duties, which meant they had to be trained on a regular basis. It was another problem of living in or near a garrison town.

ST MARY'S CLERK IN TROUBLE

In 1536 John Watwode, clerk at St Mary's, was imprisoned in Warwick Castle. He had rung the church bells on St Lawrence's Day, which was not a holy day!

EARLY SNIPER ACTION

Greville was not present at the siege, and the castle was under the command of Sir Edward Peyto. He was, however, present at the siege of Lichfield Cathedral on 2 May 1643, which was held by the Royalists. During the siege Greville was fatally shot by a musketeer. There are (unproven) suggestions that he was shot in what has been described as an early example of sniper-fire.

DAMAGE TO THE BEAUCHAMP CHAPEL

Some of the stained glass windows behind the altar in the Beauchamp Chapel look strange. In fact, it contains the remnants which survived the attentions of over-zealous Puritan troops. Fortunately the tomb of Richard Beauchamp survived, although it had already experienced serious problems in the mid-1500s. For nearly 200 years the question of whether or not his body was actually in the tomb was debated. Then, suddenly, the floor of the chapel collapsed, exposing his body inside. It looked like he was asleep. A few minutes later the body disintegrated, leaving only some of his hair behind. Local folklore has it that some of Warwick's women made it into rings...

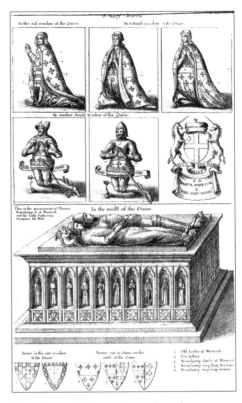

Beauchamp windows, shown above the monument of Thomas Beauchamp. (With kind permission of the Thomas Fisher Rare Book Library, University of Toronto)

AD 1687

THE MAYOR MUST DIE!

THE MAYOR WAS furious as he left Divine Service.

Yet again he – and other members of the town council – had endured a long and abusive tirade aimed at them by the incumbent of St Mary's church, the Revd William Edes.

Whilst he claimed to be a Protestant, Edes (like James II) had very strong Roman Catholic leanings. In fact, he was suspected of being a secret member of their faith. Unfortunately for the council, Edes had friends in high places and was impossible to remove. Irrespective of what the council did, Edes always found fault with it: every Sunday morning he

reminded them of their shortcomings. Leaning over the pulpit, he would harangue them – particularly the mayor.

Being councillors, they were required to attend Divine Service every Sunday, where they became a captive audience for his rants.

In June 1687 a son was born to James II and his wife. The prince was another James Stuart, and would ultimately become known as the Old Pretender. This son would cause death and misery for decades to come. Edes proudly announced at St Mary's that the boy would be brought up as a Roman Catholic. He was expecting his

CATHOLIC BISHOP ENTERTAINED

In February 1687 James II declared that there would be religious tolerance shown towards Roman Catholics and Quakers. Consequently, Edes soon became involved with the building of a new Roman Catholic chapel in the Saltisford. He insisted on putting a coin over the doorframe; in addition, he paid a workman the sum of 6d to ensure the first letter of his name was also put over the door. When Bishop Giffard came to consecrate the chapel he was entertained by Edes, who provided as much food and wine as the bishop and his priests desired.

The chapel had gone by 1737.

James II. (THP)

they were very pro-Roman Catholic in outlook. They believed the king could do no wrong, and if they were acting in his name then *they* could do no wrong. In other words they considered themselves to be above the law.

It was such an attitude which had been one of the causes of the Civil War only a few years earlier, and which would contribute to James II's downfall in 1688.

His brother's arrival now gave William Edes the support he needed in his vendetta against the mayor. (What first caused it has never been established.)

At a meeting in a local barber's shop, the brothers agreed to go and kill the mayor. Arming themselves, they went to his house in High Street, close to the Lord Leycester Hospital.

'Where is he? We've come to kill him!' they shouted.

congregation to go wild with joy at the announcement. Instead, they greeted his news with a stony silence. But Edes was undeterred: he knew what was scheduled to happen later that year.

James II was always short of money, and permanently looking for means of raising revenue. He now chose several capable and ruthless military officers and sent them into various towns with instructions to seize their charters. This would enable him to take over their income. In late 1687, just such a military party arrived in Warwick to seize the charter. They were under the command of an officious and bullying officer called Edes – William's brother. And they made a most unholy alliance. Both brothers held similar views, and

The Old Pretender, James II's son, over whom the vicar and his parishioners fought. (THP)

39

They forced their way into his house, but found only his terrified family. After a cursory search the brothers left the house ... but they were soon back again. 'Where is he?' they demanded, time and time again. 'We're not going till we've killed him!' Once again they made a cursory search of the house, and they still failed to find him. This time, when they left, they did not return.

It turned out that the mayor (feeling unwell) had gone to bed: he was there on both occasions when his house was invaded. Somehow, and much to his relief, the brothers did not find him. Had they done so, they might well have killed him. Having failed to find the mayor, the soldiers seized the charter and left town. With his brother gone, and deprived of military support, William Edes quietened down – and the mayor came out of hiding.

William Edes stayed on at St Mary's until 1706. During this time he oversaw the rebuilding of the church in the immediate post-fire era.

AD 1694

RAGING INFERNO ENGULFS TOWN

'**F**IRE! FIRE!'
Soon after 2 p.m. on 5 September 1694, those dreaded and fearful cries echoed around the streets of Warwick. They were quickly taken up by other people, and the panic spread. In a few short minutes the flames, driven by a merciless gale-force wind, quickly engulfed the town. Within a short space of time the fire had spread. In the words of an eyewitness, 'all endeavours that be could used to limit the fierceness of its progress were vain and inefficient'. During the following hours, which must have seemed like a lifetime to the hapless residents, the old market town was changed for ever.

By the time the fire was extinguished there were few people who had not been affected by it, and many who had lost everything they possessed.

NO FIRE-FIGHTING EQUIPMENT!

From its starting place opposite the Lord Leycester Hospital, the fire rapidly spread through the town, destroying almost everything in its path. The fiery monster's progress was greatly helped by the configuration and make-up of the town. Timber-framed buildings, with their thatched roofs, usually standing in narrow alleyways, were quickly consumed.

Following those initial hapless cries, Mayor Joseph Blissett quickly took charge of the fire-fighting operations. There was no regular fire brigade, and he had to use whatever volunteers he could find. It was a mammoth task, especially as one of the first casualties was Warwick's only fire engine! This was quickly followed by all the fire buckets, which were burnt. Whilst there was no shortage of water in the river, it had to be got from there to the burning town. The helpers were quickly reminded that Warwick stood on a hill! In the early stages Mayor Blissett had no shortage of volunteers ready to help, in spite of the heat and ferocity of the flames. But it was a different story once the fire spread closer to their homes: quite understandably, the volunteers abandoned what they were doing and went to salvage what few of their own possessions they could.

BUILDINGS DEMOLISHED

Mayor Blissett knew he could wait no longer. He had to make a most radical decision and implemented the recognised means of fighting fires in urban areas. He ordered the demolition of all the houses in the path of the fire which were not already burning. Fires need to feed on fuel (in this case combustible buildings). The idea was to deny the fire any more fuel: by demolishing these buildings fire breaks were created, which in turn starved the flames which slowly began to subside. His methods ultimately extinguished the blaze and saved some parts of the town. However, it was a most unpopular action, as many of the people whose houses were pulled down had nurtured the forlorn hope that the fire might burn out before it reached their homes.

Whilst the fire raged there were some notable casualties, and many acts of heroism. One specific casualty was the house which adjoined the one owned by Dr William Johnson in Smith Street, now called Landor House. This had been extensively re-vamped and modernised only a few months earlier. Only too aware of the money he stood to lose if his house was destroyed, Dr Johnson decided to embark on a drastic measure: having convinced himself that he had the mayor's permission to create a fire break, he set about pulling down his neighbour's house. The problem was that the fire stopped quite some distance away: the demolition had been totally unnecessary. Needless to say, the owner of the affected property was far from happy, and he later sued Dr Johnson for damages.

Another building which sadly did not survive the firestorm was most of St Mary's collegiate church.

The building might possibly have survived if distressed townsfolk had not sought shelter there, taking with them their most treasured possessions. Churches are accepted places of refuge in times of trouble, and the Revd Edes could not prevent people from entering – even if he had wanted to. Unfortunately for his church, some of the possessions which were carried inside were already smouldering, and they soon burst into flame. In a short time the fabric of the church was alight, and the people inside now had to flee once more for their lives. Fortunately for future generations of Warwickians and visitors to the town, James Fish, the parish clerk, acted with great presence of mind as the fire spread into the church. He was assisted only by four brave parishioners. Dodging the flames and the molten lead, which was beginning to pour down from the roof, they saved the wonderful Beauchamp Chapel. This is the burial place of Richard Beauchamp and Robert Dudley.

James Fish was not so lucky: his house was destroyed.

In a great act of humanity, all the prisoners were released from the gaol. This certainly saved their lives. Whilst some of them stayed to help fight the fire, others took advantage of the chaos and ran for it. No one can say for sure just how many of them returned.

Sadly, but inevitably, owners of many of the abandoned and ruined houses were subjected to further grief. Whenever a tragedy such as this occurs it acts as a magnet for unscrupulous sorts: they took advantage of the unguarded

ANOTHER SERIOUS WARWICK FIRE

In the early hours of Sunday, 3 December 1871, there was a disastrous fire at Warwick Castle. The cause was never fully identified, but it possibly started in her ladyship's dressing-room. There was a considerable amount of damage but no lives were lost (although two of the earl's children, and some servants, had lucky escapes).

Fortunately the main structure of the building was not seriously damaged, although the same could not be said for its interior. A new roof and much redecorating were needed, at a cost of around £100,000 (approximately £4.5 million today). Some of the treasures in the burnt rooms were irrevocably lost, although luckily no masterpieces were affected. There was great sympathy in the country for the earl and countess, who were absent at the time of the outbreak. In spite of being situated close to the River Avon, river water could not be used to fight the blaze: the castle was too high, and there was insufficient pressure to allow the water to reach the flames. Water had to be supplied from the town, all of which took extra time. Other fire appliances attended from Warwick, Leamington, Bilton Grange, Coventry and two from Birmingham. Communications were hampered because the Warwick Telegraph Office was closed!

A local artist, Mr William Fincher, was later arrested. He was charged with stealing a gold seal and snuff-box from the scene.

Queen Victoria opened a public subscription with £1,000 (approximately £45,400 today) towards the restoration of the castle.

---

property in the town and stole whatever they could.

As night finally fell on a day that would never be forgotten, the fire was extinguished (although a lingering heavy smell of burning filled the night air). Only when dawn came was the full extent of the horror fully appreciated. The only good news was that nobody had been killed.

CAUSE OF THE FIRE

It was thought the fire was caused by someone carrying a lighted taper from one building to another: a spark was blown from the taper and flew up to a thatched roof. That was all that it took for the town to be destroyed.

Fires in old towns were not at all uncommon. Their layout, coupled with the use of naked flames for heating, lighting, business and cooking purposes, made them major fire risks. Very much aware of this problem, fire insurance had been made available nationwide for the previous fourteen years. Yet no house-owners in Warwick had taken advantage of such schemes: they probably believed that it would never happen to them. But it did, and the affected householders soon came to regret their indolence.

The authorities were now faced with the mammoth task of rebuilding the town, and providing aid to its suffering residents. It was an uphill task, and it was one which would be accompanied by allegations of incompetence and corruption.

CORRUPTION OR INCOMPETENCE?

THE FIRE CAUSED real misery in the town, but this paled into insignificance compared with what happened in its aftermath.

Such fires were not uncommon in the seventeenth century. When they happened it was vital to ensure that the affected towns were rebuilt as quickly as possible. A financial bonus was offered to encourage this – and a penalty for dilatory action. Consequently, the designing of a new town was one of the top priorities which faced Mayor Joseph Blissett on the morning after the fire.

MONEY MADE FROM MISERY

The most pressing need was to find food, clothes and shelter for the homeless. Many people had lost their tools and were unable to work. There was a pressing need for instant money to be made available. Charitable donations soon began flooding into Warwick from all over the country. Meanwhile, the magistrates had to record details of all the losses sustained, and the deadline for making claims was very short.

People claiming for the loss of goods were allowed just nine days to complete their applications. Claims for loss of houses had to be made by independent assessors: although these reports were allowed more time, they still had to be submitted by 27 September. All these applications had to be made on oath. It was not a time for dithering.

Sadly, where there is misery and tragedy, there is also the opportunity to make money. Numerous stonemasons and carpenters descended on the town and began compiling their reports. No records exist on how much they charged for their valuations.

DWINDLING FUNDS

The cost of rebuilding Warwick was finally quoted at £120,000 (approximately £12,000,000 today). The figures were accepted, and an Act of Parliament was passed to this effect, but a time limit of two years was placed on the rebuilding project. A body of commissioners, under the chairmanship of the Earl of Warwick, was set up to oversee the administering of relief to

WREN'S CHURCH DESIGN SNUBBED

Many people maintained that most of the missing money had been used to rebuild St Mary's church. Regardless of the truth of such allegations, the church experienced its own problems with reconstruction. Amongst the various plans submitted were some by Christopher Wren. However, they were rejected by the crown commissioners, and the contract was given to a local architect, Sir William Wilson, who was born in Leicestershire. His design was faulty, and led to the main pillars of the new church cracking. In desperation Wilson sought help from Christopher Wren's mason, Edward Strong. Consequently, the tower is now attached to the church instead of being part of it…

the townspeople. Initially it seemed to be a very good arrangement, but the honeymoon period soon came to an end. Benefactors such as the Bishop of Worcester raised money, but it was nowhere near enough – and to make matters worse, these donations soon dwindled. Now the victims found, to their dismay, that they were not obtaining anything like the fair value of their losses. As the years passed the situation did not improve: when the accounts were closed, in 1721, there were many very unhappy people in Warwick. It was now more than twenty-six years since the fire, and claimants had been paid just four shillings in the pound for their buildings, and one shilling and sixpence in the pound for their belongings.

CORRUPTION OR INCOMPETENCE?

Accusations of corruption and incompetence soon followed – and they were never fully resolved. For example:

- One of the commissioners borrowed some guineas from the fund only a

few hours before they were devalued. Overnight he made a profit of £220 (approximately £15,500 today) – a profit which he was rumoured to have shared with the town clerk.

- Another criticism was levelled at the receiver general for taxes in Warwickshire, who was also the town clerk's father. He had been given the task of banking the donations, at a time when there was a considerable amount of clipped silver coins in circulation. In an attempt to address this problem, the government minted new coins and established a deadline for the old, bad currency to be surrendered. The receiver missed this deadline, costing the fund many hundreds of pounds.

UNHAPPY ENDING

These, and other irregularities, led to a series of bitter quarrels between the townspeople and the commissioners. When the account was finally closed, the townspeople started legal proceedings against them in the Chancery Court.

Court House. (Author's collection)

But it was to no avail.

Whilst the townspeople had a good case, they could not afford to pay the legal fees, and the proceedings were abandoned. It was a sad and unhappy ending to a long and drawn-out affair. All this misery was caused by a single spark from a lit taper more than a quarter of a century earlier. No doubt the town council heaved a big sigh of relief when the threat of court action passed, but their tranquillity would not last. The great fire had not yet ceased causing them problems...

COUNCIL CORRUPTION UNCOVERED

Having witnessed the grand houses that were now springing up, the council decided to improve its headquarters (still known as the Court House today). The building had not really been affected by the fire, but it looked shabby compared to the new houses. Unfortunately they did not have the necessary funds for the work – but that was only a minor problem for them. They used funds from the charities of Henry VIII and Sir Thomas White to illegally and corruptly pay for it. When they were found out, in 1736, the council was suspended and banned from using the Court House until all the money – £931 10s 5d – had been repaid in full. Meanwhile, the council had to meet in local inns or anywhere else that would have them. The charges against them also included 'feasting at the expense of the town', and erecting buildings that were of no use to the inhabitants, the people they were meant to serve!

It took until 1769 for the money to be repaid. On the positive side, Warwick still enjoys the Court House, created by Francis Smith.

WARWICK'S MOST SCANDALOUS RESIDENTS

THE WARWICKSHIRE POP-LOLLY

One question has never been resolved about Olive Serres, neé Wilmot (1772-1834): was she or was she not the Princess of Cumberland?

It is fair to say that her early days, spent in St John's House, Warwick, gave no indication of what would happen to her in later life. Whilst Olive was a beautiful woman and an accomplished author and publisher, she also enjoyed the less flattering reputation of being a courtesan.

Olive was born in Warwick, and at her baptism, in St Nicholas' church, it was recorded that she was the daughter of Robert and Anna Wilmot. However, she would later deny these details, maintaining that she was the niece of George III through his brother Henry's marriage to a commoner. Robert Wilmot was an artist, and if he was her father she may have obtained her artistic talent through him.

In 1780, when Robert was treasurer to the county of Warwick, he was accused of embezzlement. On being dismissed from his post, he and his family were evicted from St John's House.

Olive went to live with her uncle James at the Barton-on-the-Heath vicarage. Whilst she was there the vicarage was robbed. Olive appeared to be the heroine of the night after she raised the alarm. Later it was rumoured she had been in league with the robbers, two of whom were hanged. Soon afterwards she moved to London.

It was the start of her notoriety.

After a disastrous marriage to John Thomas Serres, Olive indulged in various affairs and had an illegitimate son. It did not take long for her to acquire the nickname of 'the Warwickshire Pop-Lolly', meaning a sweetmeat but with obviously lewd overtones.

St John's House. (Author's collection)

In time she became friendly with George Greville, the impoverished 2nd Earl of Warwick (following the title's re-creation in 1759). When his debts became too heavy he was evicted from the castle, and trustees put in charge of the estate. During this time Olive supported him financially. Although a noble idea, it seriously backfired: he passed a 'bill of exchange' (the forerunner of the cheque) which bounced, and she was imprisoned for debt. In view of what happened later, did she have an ulterior motive in helping the earl?

Another friendship she enjoyed was with the Duke of Kent, who had wanted to marry her. The problem was that she already had a husband.

Gradually she heard rumours concerning her apparent true birth. It was said that her real father was not Robert Wilmot, but Henry Frederick, Duke of Cumberland. Her mother was also known as Olive, but with no surname recorded. Henry was George III's youngest brother, and usually considered to be the worst of the siblings. Often referred to as 'the royal idiot', he was renowned for his numerous mistresses. Following one particular affair (and believed marriage), George III exiled him – although he returned to England in due course. If Olive Serres had been born in wedlock then she was of royal blood and could be addressed as 'the Princess of Cumberland'. And if this was true, she was in the line of succession to the throne. Needless to say, members of the royal family were not impressed by such news. Who was this woman? Where was the proof for her claims?

In 1820, Olive opened letters she had been given by the Earl of Warwick. She had promised not to read them until after George III's death. Having read their contents, Olive became convinced that she was indeed of royal blood, and insisted on being addressed as 'Princess Olive'. She maintained she had been so created in 1773 by George III. There seems to be little doubt that this happened, although the royal family did not openly welcome her. If she was not a royal, why was she permitted to drive in a carriage which displayed the royal coat of arms? (Her new-found royal status, however, did not prevent her from being imprisoned for debt on several occasions.)

Undeterred by the royal family's attitude towards her, Olive campaigned to have her true status recognised. She hoped that having an affair with Joseph W. Parkins, who was sheriff of the City of London, would help her. Whilst he might have been something of an eccentric, he did not take kindly to lending her money which was never repaid. Consequently they quarrelled, and soon afterwards she jilted him in favour of a much younger man. This was a serious mistake: Olive had made a dangerous and vindictive enemy in Parkins, and he was determined to have his revenge.

Firstly he wrote to Olive's husband and complained about the machinations of 'your wicked and worthless wife'. Much to his surprise, John Serres agreed with his assessment. He added, 'it is high time such fraudulent humbug should be ... put a stop to'. Serres was also aware that the royal family had begun an enquiry to

ROYAL MARRIAGES ACT (1772)

As a result of the sexual antics of various members of the royal family during the mid to latter part of the eighteenth century, Parliament passed the Royal Marriages Act in 1772. This legislation limited the succession to the throne of England to legitimate descendants of Sophie of Hanover. Was it just coincidence that this legislation was enacted the same year in which Olive was born?

prove or disprove Olive's allegations, and he was more than happy to help them. The commissioners eventually decided that Olive's documentary proof (the letters) was a forgery. Furthermore, they decreed that she was either an impudent imposter or the innocent dupe of others. However unwilling Olive might have been to accept that decision, it was the end of the road for her hopes. She spent the next few years persisting in her allegations in between bouts of imprisonment for her debts.

One of Olive's biggest hurdles in trying to prove her case was the wild and often malicious allegations she made about members of the royal family. These tales included allegations that George IV had stabbed a groom to death; that the Duke of Kent committed adultery with his own sister; and that the Duke of Clarence had murdered two men. And to cap these were her tales about George III, which varied from him being a thief to having a 'criminal connection with his niece and his sister-in-law on a couch'.

Following Olive's death in 1834, her daughter called herself Princess Lavinia and began the petition anew. She also failed in her attempt to be recognised as being a member of the royal family.

THE GREAT SCHOLAR

Often called a great scholar, Dr Samuel Parr (1747-1825) was the cleric at Hatton for forty years, and a great champion of civil rights and religious liberty. He regularly visited Warwick Gaol, and advocated reform of the criminal code. For instance, he proposed that the death penalty should only be used for murder and treason.

Towards the end of his life Samuel became chaplain to Queen Caroline, George IV's estranged wife. Ignoring a government decree to omit her name in church services, he found a prayer which had been missed by the edict and took great delight in including her name in Divine Service whenever he could. Caroline was very popular with the ordinary people, and when proceedings

Samuel Parr.
(THP)

against her under the Pains and Penalties Bill were abandoned, there were great celebrations throughout the country. Warwick was one of the many towns which celebrated. George IV was, by contrast, incredibly unpopular in the county.

SARAH SIDDON AT GUY'S CLIFFE

Guy's Cliffe House has been occupied since early Saxon times, although the current house was built much later.

By 1751 it belonged to the Greatheed family, who later employed Sarah Kemble as a lady's maid. Although she came from a theatrical family, her parents were not keen for her to follow them. In 1773 Sarah eloped from here, married William Siddons, and ultimately became Sarah Siddons, the famous Shakespearian actress. Her acting career was not always plain sailing, and she had to work hard to succeed. In time she became a regular visitor to Guy's Cliffe House, and George Greville, 2nd Earl of Warwick, was her most steadfast patron.

Guy's Cliffe House. (Author's collection)

Post-1945, the house was scheduled to become a hotel, but it never happened. Five years later the roof and other fittings were sold, and the house soon decayed.

It was used in the 1992 television version of *Sherlock Holmes and the Last Vampyre*. The script required the ruins of the house to be set alight, albeit in a controlled manner. Unfortunately, the fire took charge and more damage was done than intended. Today the ruins are owned by the Freemasons, who use the chapel.

THIS LAMBE NOT FOR THE SLAUGHTER

Dr William Lambe (1765-1848) was born and educated in Hereford, before qualifying as a medical doctor at St John's College, Cambridge. In 1794 William moved to Warwick, where he married Harriet Mary Welsh. Described as a respected and diligent doctor, he took over Dr Walter Landor's medical practice.

We know that Dr Landor practiced in Smith Street, where his son Walter was born. Today the building is part of King's High School. However, no records exist to tell us where William lived.

Everyone liked Harriet Lambe: Dr Landor was one of her devoted fans. Friends and family were devastated when she died, of scarlet fever, quickly followed by one of her children.

William soon specialised in studying the harmful effects of drinking water, and his studies ultimately benefitted nearby Leamington Spa. Although spa water had been in the area for many years, it was now starting to grow in

THE PRODIGAL SON

Dr Walter Landor had a son who was one of the most scandalous men in Warwickshire's history. 'So long as I write in Latin, I can say what I want, and they will not be able to sue me for libel,' he once said. These few words sum up the contempt in which Walter Savage Landor (1775-1864) held most people.

Born in 1775, in one of the best houses in Warwick, his future should have been assured – but that was not to be the case. Young Walter soon displayed a headstrong nature, which his family tolerated as 'high spirits'. Had his disobedience been tackled then, his later life might have been very different. Instead, Walter was allowed to develop his high-handed approach to all levels of authority. Walter was initially sent to a boarding school about 8 miles away from home. From there he went to Rugby School (instead of the closer Warwick School). This decision was to be Rugby's bad luck and very much Warwick's good fortune. At Rugby he quickly mastered Latin – and no one was safe from his vitriolic writings from that point on. Amongst his victims was the headmaster. Walter was expelled from school – not that it worried him.

His next excursion into education was at Trinity College, Oxford. His new targets included just about every person who had some sort of standing in society. Although a firm believer in the pen being mightier than the sword, he was quite prepared to use violence if he felt the need justified it: taking great exception to someone who held opposite political views to his own, Walter shot the man's windows out.

Here is an example of his written insults, with a heavily slanted political angle:

> George the First was always reckoned
> Viler was George the Second:
> And what mortal ever heard
> Any good of George the Third?
> But when from earth the Fourth descend
> God be praised the Georges end.

The authorities were not impressed, and it was goodbye to Oxford for Walter. Officially it was only for a year, but he never returned to his studies.

He quarrelled for the rest of his life with friends, tenants and the authorities. Always a restless individual, Walter also travelled round Europe, leaving a wake of law cases behind him. Once he was accused of being a spy for the Prince of Wales and of threatening government officials. He treated most of these allegations with disdain, but he came unstuck in Florence during 1829 when he produced another of his written tirades in Latin – easily understood, of course, in Italy. He was banished.

He truly was Savage by name and savage by nature.

---

popularity. William set out to prove how beneficial drinking such water was to the imbiber. This was all at a time when the full impact of water-borne diseases was not understood: diseases were thought to come from smells and, with very few exceptions, no one was concerned about the water they consumed. Cholera and all manner of stomach ills were accepted as a fact of life (and death). However, just imagine the effects of drinking water with human and animal sewage mixed with it. Diarrhoea, vomiting, itching, weight loss and blood poisoning were but a few of the symptoms. It was not unusual for people to vomit, urinate and defecate into the same water supply, and such a state of affairs would persist until the late 1840s before these problems were properly tackled.

Although he was recognised as being an intelligent and an accomplished physician, Lambe's views were not universally accepted. Initially he concentrated on the injurious effects of drinking water which had been taken straight from source. And his theories were based on fact: he could prove that pure water was good for treating gout and dysentery. And that wasn't all. He often stated that 'clearness, beauty of complexion, muscular strength and fullness of habit free from grossness,' could be attained by drinking pure water.

Throughout his long life Lambe campaigned continually about the dangers to be found in untreated water, in addition to the lead pipes used on pumps. He was particularly concerned about water coming straight from any source which was shared by animals. In his opinion, fetid animal oil in water was passed on to the drinkers, which made them smell. It also resulted in them having 'offensive smells to their secretions'. As expected, William's critics considered him to be an eccentric, and rubbished his ideas. But he had the last laugh when he was able to prove that all river water contained impurities, such as animal or vegetable matter, which could be harmful to the drinker.

Spa water well. (Author's collection)

In many parts of the world, the main water supply to a community also included their waste-disposal scheme, which made it a disaster waiting to happen. He was keen to promote the idea of drinking spa waters, which did not come straight from a river, and were therefore safer to drink.

By 1806 William had moved to London, where he became very concerned with his own health. He rightly believed that water drawn from the Thames was of a very dubious quality. From now on, he only drank distilled water, to which he added pure plant and fruit juice. As water cost one penny a gallon to distil, but sold at four pennies a gallon, he preferred to distil his own. Going to Malvern for pure water was not an option for him. He prescribed drinking distilled water for the removal of black crusts from teeth, and for the correction of offensive smells and secretions!

Following his own ill-health, William changed his diet. The actual illness was not recorded but its symptoms were described as being 'violent'. Meat now became a definite no-no for him, and it was the same diet he recommended for his patients. He practiced what he preached: 'My reason for objecting to every species of matter to be used as food, except the direct produce of the earth, is founded on the broad ground that no other matter is suited for the organs of man, and includes eggs, milk, cheese and fish.' One of his patients was Percy Bysshe Shelley, once described as a nineteenth-century hippie, who supported William's ideas and often wrote about them, particularly their

The grave of Shelley, Dr Lambe's most famous patient. (Giovanni Dall'Orto)

shared interest in vegetarianism. One such example was called *On the Crime of Committing Cruelty on Brutes; and on Sacrificing them to the Purposes of Man.*

For breakfast, Lambe ate only raw potatoes mixed with olive oil. At other times he ate a vegetable pudding, pie or onion dumplings. But there were problems with the vegetable puddings: butter was needed to make the pastry!

Unsurprisingly, he nearly always dined alone.

Whilst he was considered to be the perfect gentleman, he insisted that his family complied with his instructions. Once his children had married and left home they tended to go their own way when it came to food. On one occasion, when he arrived unexpectedly, the family was eating some ham: they quickly piled it up onto another plate, explaining that it was for the governess.

His treatments were recommended for the treatment of consumption, scrofula and asthma. 'Eat what you fancy, and as much as you can without distension. Abstain from animal foods, fermented drinks and impure water,' he said.

William always walked everywhere, and he never rode. On his death, aged seventy-two, he was described as being a tall man who was in better health than he had been at forty. He never went anywhere without his pamphlets, and never lost any opportunity to hand them out.

He well deserves being recognised as 'the father of vegan nutrition'.

JAMES MORISON'S CURE-ALL VEGETABLE PILLS

A contemporary of William Lambe who believed in the use of vegetables, albeit in a different context, was James Morison, a quack doctor. (A quack is another name for a cheat: these doctors sold alternative medicines, many of which contained poison.)

Morison believed that 'bad blood' was the cause of all disease, and this led him to create his own 'cure-all vegetable pills'. These pills, he insisted, were harmless – and the more one took, the quicker they worked! But they could, and often did, cause violent bowel movements. Sometimes these were fatal, though Morison was always very careful to put the blame on the apothecary who had made up the pills in these cases. The medical profession loathed him, and regularly lampooned his pills by producing caricatures of people turning into vegetables after taking them. When he died Morison was a very wealthy man, and his vegetable pills continued to sell for several years after his death.

WIFE FOR SALE!

On 18 March 1825, Lydia Harvey, from Leamington, had a notice published concerning reports in the *Warwick and Warwickshire Advertiser* claiming that she had been sold in Warwick Market the previous week. Her husband James was blamed for spreading the reports. She also referred to the other false rumours being circulated about her which she considered as being injurious to her character. Her letter denied all the allegations, maintaining that she had not left home that day. She insisted the allegations were totally false and had been spread by her malicious enemies. Lydia was employed as a washerwoman, and she pleaded with her customers not to move their business elsewhere. Had the reports really been spread by her husband, or by her rivals?

HARASSMENT OF DR WAKE

During the middle of June 1826 Warwick and Leamington were much annoyed by the activities of Mary Ann Wassell, described as a 'well-dressed woman' of more than forty.

She was involved in a Chancery Court case concerning the late Mr Pinfold's estate. Wassell alleged that the estate owed her money which the deceased had borrowed from her. In support of her case she produced a written note, allegedly signed by him, confirming the debt, although the relatives denied that the writing was his. Dr Wake from Warwick had attended Mr Pinfold and was believed to have a sample of his handwriting – but he said he could not find it!

Wassell did not believe him. Furious with his inability to help her, she began following him everywhere he went, continually pestering him. On 9 June Wassell followed him and his family to the circus at Castle Street. She was accompanied by a mob some 200-300 strong, which continually shouted 'Head him! Head him!' In desperation, Dr Wake appealed to the constables for protection and Wassell was arrested. When she appeared in court she denied causing a breach of the peace. Nonetheless, as she could not find sureties for her good behaviour Wassell was sentenced to three months' imprisonment, and had to be forcibly removed from the court. It seemed she was known to the governor of the gaol, and had a previous conviction for a similar offence in Norfolk. A month later she tried to challenge the legality of the court in order to revoke her sentence. She failed.

St Nicholas' church. (Author's collection)

SCANDALOUS BEHAVIOUR STOPS WEDDING

On 9 July 1826, a young couple's wedding at St Nicholas' church was stopped by the vicar because of the scandalous behaviour of the groom at the altar. Instead of plighting his troth, as custom decrees, he burst into a fit of uncontrollable laughter. Although the vicar gave him every opportunity to stop laughing, he continued to do so. The vicar finally stopped the ceremony – which was completed the next day, with a very chastened groom.

Nobody knew what he had found so funny.

Castle Street. (Author's collection)

Racecourse. (Author's collection)

RACECOURSE RIOT

On 3 September 1826, in the early evening, several drunk and quarrelsome individuals overturned gambling tables at the racecourse. They then broke the legs off the tables to use as weapons.

From there, they proceeded to break down the gaming tents, and destroyed the silk and canvas which covered them. The police, under the leadership of Thomas Bellerby, became involved and finally quelled the riot, but only after some very desperate fighting had taken place and many persons had been seriously injured.

Seven rioters were arrested.

AD 1809

NO HONOUR AMONG THIEVES

'**N**OW!' CRIED THE leader of the four men, as the lone traveller came into sight on the Stratford Road.

The man still had several miles to travel and he was thinking about getting out of the cold January night. Being robbed was not what he had planned for the evening.

William Garner was suddenly shaken out of his reverie by the shout as the gang rushed out of hiding and caught hold of his horse. Moments later he was pulled roughly out of the saddle and onto the ground. Taken by surprise, he was unable to defend himself and offered no resistance. Nevertheless, the footpads kicked him and beat him with their fists.

'Keep still!' snarled their leader, as he searched his victim's pockets. In a matter of moments William's money and silver watch were gone. Whilst that was happening, other members of the gang had taken the saddle off his horse and thrown it into the bushes. Slapping the already frightened animal on its rump, they sent the beast off towards Longbridge, where it was later recovered.

The cowardly attack happened between 7 p.m. and 8 p.m. on Friday 13 January. It was not Mr Garner's lucky day.

Nearly twenty-four hours later, the gang struck again at Stank Hill. Their victims were Edward Avern and Thomas Floyd, who were travelling home after having been at the market.

Suddenly four footpads, all described as wearing smocks, leapt out of the shadows. Without any warning, one of the villains – undoubtedly their leader – fired his pistol and shot Mr Avern, who fell forward. Luckily he was not too badly hurt and managed to stay in his saddle. Already frightened by the shot, his horse needed no urging to gallop away. Later, more than twenty pellets were removed from the injured man's hip. Before his hapless companion could react, he was pulled off his horse and onto the ground. Like the unfortunate William Garner, he too was kicked and beaten into submission, before being robbed of his money.

Once he had recovered sufficiently, Thomas Floyd returned to Warwick and found the night watch. The mayor took charge of the hunt for the robbers. Undoubtedly these were the same four men who had attacked William Garner

HAZARD FOR WARWICK TRAVELLER

———— ∾∾∾ ————

In 1912 William Argylle left 14 Mill Street, Warwick, for America, but he never arrived. He had sailed aboard the *Titanic*.

———— ∾∾∾ ————

the previous night. Within the week a reward of more than 300 guineas (approximately £10,000 today) had been offered for information leading to their arrests and convictions. As an additional carrot, any of the gang who 'shopped his accomplices' would also be entitled to the reward, and a possible pardon too. (It was made very clear that this offer did not apply to the individual who had shot Mr Avern.)

But it was all to no avail.

A few days later a sheep was stolen from Priory Park, and interest in the highway robberies waned – at least for the time being...

In mid-July the case was suddenly and dramatically re-opened. A prisoner serving time in the county gaol asked to see the governor, Henry Tatnall, on a matter of some importance concerning the robberies. Once he was convinced the man was telling the truth, Mr Tatnall went to the mayor and action was taken.

At that particular moment, Private William Bryan and Sergeant Patrick Wickham, both from the 103rd Regiment of Foot (disbanded in 1817), were identified as being responsible for the robberies. The two men were arrested, just before the assizes sat, and they appeared in that calendar. In 1809 highway robbery was a capital offence. This was still a time when a judge had

the power to sentence felons to hang, and then reprieve them if he wished at the end of the sitting. However, this was not an option open to Wickham, identified as the man who had fired the shot. Conscious of this, William Bryan needed little persuasion to abandon the creed of honour among thieves and turn King's Evidence, and he testified against Wickham. It was a wise move on his part and undoubtedly saved his life.

But there was still another surprise to come.

Both men were further charged with having stolen the sheep from Priory Park just after the robberies. They had brought the animal into town, where it was secretly killed and salted down. Its head, skin and entrails had been thrown into a privy.

At the assizes, the judge had no compunction in sentencing Wickham to death, as the law required. It was a popular verdict, although the condemned man no doubt thought differently. He knew there would be little or no chance of any reprieve... and he was right.

On 18 August 1809, Patrick Wickham kept his appointment with the hangman on the scaffold outside Warwick Gaol. He was aged twenty-four at the time of his execution.

The fate of the other members of the gang was not recorded.

TRIAL BY COMBAT

The Strange Case of Abraham Thornton

'**N**OT GUILTY!' REPLIED the foreman of the jury in answer to the clerk of the court's question.

A hostile silence greeted his response. Most people present at the Warwick Assizes shook their heads in total disbelief at the verdict. Among them was William Ashford, who glowered at the thickset Abraham Thornton as he left the dock. Thornton had just been on trial for murdering William's sister Mary.

On 20 May 1817, only a few weeks earlier, Mary Ashford, who lived near Castle Bromwich, went to a dance at Erdington, then in Warwickshire. Her main dancing partner for the evening was Abraham Thornton, who fancied himself a ladies' man. During the evening Thornton had boasted to friends that he would 'have Mary before

morning'. His words were remembered, and they had dire consequences. Mary was last seen alive at about 5 a.m. the next morning. Two hours later, her body was found in a water-filled pit. 'I saw some blood about forty yards from that pit, below the gate,' testified William Lavell at the trial. 'And about fourteen yards up, nearer the pit, I traced that train of blood for fourteen yards; it ran straight towards the pit, across the path on the clover.'

James Simmons added that he 'afterwards went home and fetched a rake and some long reins, and came back and dragged for the body; and after throwing the rake into the water three or four times, we dragged out the body of Mary Ashford ... there was a little mud and some old oak leaves about the face.'

In June 1819 both 'appeal of murder' and 'wager of battel' were repealed in English law, but they remained within the European Union until 2002. There is a suggestion that Sir Walter Scott may have read about this affair, giving him the idea for the wager-by-battel scene in his novel *Ivanhoe*.

THE STRANGEST DUEL

A duel was reportedly fought in medieval France between a man and a dog. Some time previously, the dog's master had been murdered. The man was suspected, but there was no human who could testify against him: the dog was the only witness. Confident that he could beat a dog, the man agreed to fight the animal armed only with a stick. Unfortunately for the murderer, the dog won the combat. Under the rules of engagement the man was considered to be guilty of the murder and executed.

The famous duel: man vs dog.

Her arms were bruised, and there was blood between her legs. A medical examination confirmed that sexual intercourse had taken place. Had she been a virgin? Or was it the onset of her period?

The popular belief was that she had been raped and murdered – and Abraham Thornton was the number-one suspect. He was quickly arrested, despite his protestations that he was innocent, and conveyed to Warwick Gaol.

In due course he appeared for trial at the assizes, on charges of murder and rape.

Feelings against him had been high from the moment of his arrest, and they continued in the run-up to the trial. It was considered an 'open and shut case', and no one expected an acquittal. In fact, they looked forward to seeing him hanged.

It took ten hours for all the witnesses to be heard. For the most part, the main prosecution evidence concerned Thornton's movements that morning. In 1817 England did not have a standard time, and communities set their clocks to whatever time they thought was appropriate. Standard time would not come in until the railways arrived. The case would stand or fall on this factor.

According to the evidence, Thornton had been seen near to where Mary's body was found. However, the problem with the timing of these sightings, if they were correct, was that he had only a space of eleven minutes to assault and murder Mary and then to walk 3 miles. It would be an impossible task for a practised runner, which Thornton clearly was not. And he had no access to a horse.

Consequently, he was found not guilty on both charges.

Much to everyone's dismay and disgust, Thornton was discharged. That should have been the end of the matter – but it was not to be. The newspapers kept the case alive, and they were delighted when William Ashford, Mary's brother, moved to call a second trial. Thornton was re-arrested on an 'appeal of murder', instigated by William Ashford. This was an old law which allowed him to take out a private prosecution against Thornton. The new trial was opened at the King's Bench division in London, where William received a rather unpleasant shock, something which neither he nor anyone else had anticipated. When the charge was put to Thornton, he replied: 'Not guilty – and I am ready to defend the same with my body.' As he spoke, Mr Reader (Thornton's lawyer) handed his client a pair of large gauntlets. Thornton put one of them on and threw the other down for William to pick up, thereby challenging him to 'wager of battel'.

POTTY PARSON MURDERS MAID!

Murder was also stalking the streets of Warwick in this era. When Hannah Miller (fourteen), servant to Mr George the butcher, started work on 5 March 1812, no one knew she would be dead before teatime. Mr George had premises opposite the Lord Leycester Hospital. His lodger was the Revd William Brookes, known to all as 'Mad Brookes'. For no apparent reason Brookes shot Hannah in her neck and back. Although she received immediate attention from local physician Mr Blenkinsop, she died shortly afterwards. When Brookes was tried at the assizes for murder the court found him unfit to plead, and he was detained indefinitely.

This sentence was in complete contrast to the case of Ann Heytree, convicted in 1819, who maintained she had been instructed by voices to murder her mistress. She too was clearly 'unfit to plead', but she did not have the same influential friends that Brookes had. She was hanged at Warwick later that same year.

Lord Leycester Hospital. (Author's collection)

William did not pick it up.

Everyone in court was taken completely by surprise by this twist. 'Wager of battel' (as it was known and spelt) demanded that the case be settled by way of trial by combat. This outmoded practice was still on the statute book, although it had not been used in England since 1446. Thornton was within his legal rights, and his claim could not be denied. It meant that the two men would fight, with wooden clubs, from sunrise to sunset, or until one of them had been killed or surrendered. Should Thornton be unable to continue, then he would be immediately hanged. And there was little chance of that happening: he was far stronger than his opponent.

It was a simple choice for William: accept Thornton's challenge, or withdraw his case. His only hope was that the judge would not agree to the wager. However, the judge was unsure of what to do, and he adjourned the case so that he could take advice. It dragged on until February 1818, when the judge ruled that he had to act in accordance with the law. And that meant the conditions of the 'wager of battel' were legal, and must take place unless William declined to accept the challenge. Heart-broken, William instructed his counsel to drop the appeal of murder. In return, Thornton withdrew his challenge of 'wager of battel'. Thornton was released. Only too aware of his unpopularity, he finally settled in America.

Nobody was ever convicted for Mary's murder.

RADICAL RECTOR REFUSED ENTRY TO OWN CHURCH!

ARTHUR SAVAGE WADE was born at Warwick, in 1787, becoming interested in politics from an early age, probably following in his father's footsteps.

In 1811 Arthur became vicar of St Nicholas' church, Warwick. For those who knew him it was a strange choice of career, as he was a Chartist and highly – and openly – critical of how the Church hierarchy acted. Perhaps he thought the only way to reform it was to join it? As a fully committed Chartist, Arthur supported:

a) Universal suffrage
b) No property qualifications for Members of Parliament
c) Annual Parliaments
d) Equal electoral districts
e) Payment of Members of Parliament
f) Voting by secret ballot

The nineteenth-century parliamentary system was corrupt, and numerous lords of the manor continued to influence who was elected to it. Without a secret ballot, everybody who mattered knew who had voted and for what party.

Having the Earl of Warwick as a close neighbour must have made for interesting times! Being just outside the castle, St Nicholas is sometimes referred to as the Castle Church.

Arthur joined the Birmingham Political Union on its inception in 1830. The Union's aims were similar to those of the Chartists, except that Thomas Attwood, their leader, insisted on using non-violent means to obtain them. The passage of the Great Reform Bill of 1832 was not without its problems, and at one stage it seemed likely to be withdrawn. Rising to the challenge, the Birmingham Political Union held an impressive gathering of over 150,000 people. Attwood made it quite clear that he could raise similar numbers of people, in different places, all at an hour's notice. Parliament had been warned. Faced with such opposition, the Bill's objectors had no alternative but to agree to its enactment. Arthur would almost certainly have been involved in this demonstration.

In 1833, following the rioting and unrest during the Warwick elections of 1831 and 1832, Arthur received

Chartist riot at Newport. (THP)

permission to move away from his parish. Officially he had heart trouble. However, there can be little doubt that he had clashed with the Earl of Warwick on too many occasions, especially during the elections. Undoubtedly it was a good idea for him to leave the town for a while. Nevertheless, it did not mean he was taking a backwards step: far from it! In next to no time he was involved with more radical theories and ideas.

Arthur now concentrated his activities in London, where he was a regular speaker at meetings. He was more than happy to address any organisation which supported and promoted his views.

Needless to say, such radical activities did not endear him to the government. They were very mindful of what had happened in France in 1789, and were scared something similar might be repeated in England, where there was no shortage of radical societies. Consequently, the government was determined to take whatever action was necessary to stop any rebellions from starting – and some of their measures were questionable, to say the least! Meanwhile, the Swing Riots had started (which caused massive unrest in the countryside, albeit mostly in Southern and Western England).

Although mainly active in 1830, there were further outbreaks in the following years. This period saw many battles between land-owners and the agricultural labourers. Then matters came to an infamous head in late February 1834, at the little Dorset village of Tolpuddle. Six agricultural labourers were arrested for swearing what was considered to be an illegal oath when they joined a union. Controversy still surrounds the circumstances of their arrest: were they set up? Were they betrayed?

What is known for definite is that a whole army of government spies, informers and *agents provocateurs* operated in England at this time. All of the 'Tolpuddle Martyrs' were found guilty, and each sentenced to seven years' transportation. Their sentences caused an immediate outcry of protest. Newspapers, of all political persuasions, attacked the verdict. Numerous protest marches were held – and Arthur was soon in his element, taking a leading role at meetings. He was already well known to the Establishment, and regarded as a subversive. No one was surprised when he was appointed chaplain to the London trade unions. But for the government this was a step too far, and it acted.

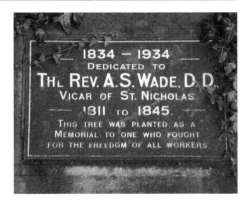

Plaque. (Author's collection)

NOT WANTED IN WARWICK

In May 1834, the government ensured that Arthur was forbidden to preach. But it was unable to stop his radical activities: along with many others, he continued ceaselessly fighting for justice for the Tolpuddle Martyrs. By now the government was fighting a losing battle. King William IV had become involved, and in 1836 he signed a royal pardon for them. No doubt Arthur would have taken part in the subsequent celebrations. With his work done, Arthur went back to Warwick, intending to take up his parish duties once more. But it was not to be. On his first visit to St Nicholas' church, he found the curate and parishioners would not let him enter (let alone conduct any services). He had made too many influential enemies.

Whilst it was a terrible blow to him, Arthur was not someone to take adversity lying down. He now concentrated on ministering to the needs of the working classes. His health began to fail at this time, and he died in 1845.

In 1934, on the centenary of the Tolpuddle Martyrs' court case, a willow tree was planted in St Nicholas' churchyard, and is dedicated to his memory. The commemorative plaque reminds people how Arthur fought for the freedom of all workers.

SCANDALOUS CHARTER

It was fortunate that Arthur was no longer alive in 1848, when the Chartist Movement, which he had supported so ardently, collapsed. A massive petition had been presented to Parliament, but was found to contain all manner of fake signatures (including those of Queen Victoria and the Duke of Wellington). The movement did not survive the ridicule that resulted.

SATAN SIGHTED IN THE STREETS

'HELP! HELP!' SCREECHED the old woman as she stumbled up the rock. 'Help! Help! The Devil is after me!'

This cry was heard in Warwick's streets in 1823. At first the night watchman was sceptical as the old woman unfolded her tale: 'I had just been to the ale house for my usual generous portion of October in a china mug, when he embraced me with more warmth than was agreeable,' she said. 'Then he threw me down and broke my mug. Then he took a hasty but affectionate farewell of me and left.' The only description she could give was that 'he was at least six feet high and dressed in dark clothes.'

The woman was known to like her drink, but he went through the motions of being interested. Meanwhile – and unbeknown to him – the Devil had only just begun his visit to Warwick. It was reported that the figure 'had gone to St John's with all the gravity of a judge, unmolested and unmolesting ... and displaying his talents, of one minute waltzing on his hind legs and then running on four.' Reports of sightings began coming in thick and fast. The Devil was in St John's, where he had taken up position by the brook and was helping travellers to cross it. (Their gratitude soon changed to panic when they saw their helper's hairy face, fierce white fangs and smelt his foetid breath.) It was clear that the very Devil himself was abroad in the streets of Warwick!

Panic took over. Whilst the watchmen conferred with each other, trying to

CRUEL SPORTS IN WARWICK

In February 1814 magistrates in Warwickshire led the way in banning the cruel activity of 'throwing at cocks'. A game cock was tied to a pole on Shrove Tuesday, and competitors threw missiles at the poor creature. The sport ended when the bird was killed. Whoever threw the winning missile claimed the bird as the prize.

SATAN SEIZES LYING LANDLORD

According to a popular piece of folklore, this was not the first time that Satan had been sighted in Warwick. Following the Battle of Edgehill in October 1642, parliamentarian soldier Jeremiah Stone came to Warwick to recover from his wounds. He stayed at the Anchor Inn, and gave the landlord his valuables for safekeeping. When he had recovered, Jeremiah asked for his valuables to be returned, only to have the landlord deny he had ever been given them. During the ensuing fracas, Jeremiah was arrested and thrown into gaol to await trial at the next assizes. On the eve of his trial he was visited by the Devil, who offered him freedom in return for his immortal soul. Jeremiah declined the offer. Surprisingly, the Devil was so impressed that he gave him specific advice: acting on these instructions, Jeremiah the next day chose the lawyer wearing a red hat. During his trial the landlord was called to give evidence, and again denied having been given the valuables. 'May the Devil come and seize me if I have told a lie,' he stressed. Before he had finished speaking, the lawyer threw off his red hat and revealed he was the Devil. He seized the lying landlord. After flying around the Market Place, the pair vanished, and the landlord was never seen again. However, the two left behind what was described as 'a terrible stinke'…

decide what to do, they were suddenly faced with another unique event which provided the answer to their problem. Earlier that evening a man and his servant had obtained lodgings at the King's Head in the Saltisford. The man had a room inside the inn, whilst his servant was lodged in an outhouse, guarding their most valuable property. They had travelled a long way, and being tired had soon bedded down for the night. Sometime before midnight, two ne'er-do-wells went snooping around the back of the King's Head and its outhouses, undoubtedly looking for something to steal. When they entered the outhouse, where the servant was sleeping, they disturbed the valuable property he was guarding: it was a prized dancing bear, which was not pleased at being woken up and reacted accordingly. The two trespassers were still blissfully unaware of their danger until the bear

'saluted one of them with a most ardent though unwelcome embrace. The fellow roared out as Bruin hugged him most vehemently.' Luckily for the man in question, he was released unharmed. Like the woman on the Rock, however, he was firmly convinced that 'his Satanic Majesty had taken possession of him'. Luckily for him, and the old woman, the bear was muzzled.

The man's partner-in-crime had wasted no time in leaving his friend to his fate and making good his own escape. The bear's victim lay on the floor, recovering from the ordeal, but as he soon discovered his problems were not yet over for the night. Both the bear's owner and the servant had been woken by the noise. However, the animal's owner did not want the night-watchmen involved, so he and his servant meted out their own summary justice to the intruder. After they had let the battered man go, they went to settle the bear down – only to find that in the hubbub the animal had vanished! They moved towards the Rock and the town centre, hoping to find traces of the missing bear.

These were not long in coming.

PANIC IN THE STREETS!

They had not gone very far before they heard the screeches coming from the Rock. By the time they arrived, the bear had gone: all they found was an old woman consuming tots of gin and regaling everyone who would listen with ever-wilder accounts of how she had survived her encounter with the Devil.

They soon found the night-watchmen and explained what had happened. Heaving great sighs of relief that they were no longer dealing with Satan, the watchmen still had a problem: how were they going to catch a bear, in the middle of the night, in Warwick? They need not have worried, as the word had already spread about what was happening. In a few minutes, 'they left the field in possession of some new-fledged nimrods, who followed the chase with unmitigated ardour until two o'clock in the morning.'

As the night progressed towards dawn, the hunt continued. Every reported sighting of the bear was investigated by shouting men and barking dogs. After a hard chase of four hours, in which the bear was by turns pursuer and pursued, he was at length 'taken by his keeper in Mr Russell's field, opposite Emscote Mill, but not before he had given one of his pursuers the hug fraternal for the marked attention and civility which he had paid him in the course of the midnight excursion.'

Warwick's great bear hunt was over, and everyone had enjoyed a good night's sport.

AD 1825

FIGHT CLUB

The Great Gun of Windsor Silenced and the Fighting Lions

A PRIZE FIGHT between Tom Cannon and Jem Ward had been planned to take place at the Factory Yard in Warwick, a popular location for all kinds of sporting events. The yard held about 15,000 spectators, and the organisers stood to make a considerable amount of money.

Such events were officially illegal, so magistrates were tasked with preventing them from happening whilst the organisers tried to keep one step ahead by moving the venues. Both sides were used to this cat and mouse game. In reality this violent recreational pastime had a very large following of spectators from all social classes. However, it was the gentry and the nobility who came up with the money. For this particular contest the prize was 1,000 guineas (approximately £48,000 today) – and the promoters were determined it would go ahead.

Unlike today's boxing matches, these were very bloody affairs, fought with bare knuckles and very few rules. The bloodier the contest, the more the spectators liked it. It was not unknown for pugilists to die from the injuries they received during such contests.

Both contestants made their way to Warwick on the Sunday. Jem Ward, otherwise known as the Black Diamond, stayed at the Warwick Arms. He had not long been back on the prize-fighting scene, having been banned from fighting until 1823 for match rigging. Tom Cannon, otherwise known as the Great Gun of Windsor, was the reigning heavyweight prize-fighting champion of England. He was a force to be reckoned with, and he stayed at the Swan.

As the day progressed, coaches arrived from London, Cheltenham, Coventry and Birmingham. These were described as being 'loaded in and out' – hundreds of people were flocking to see the fight. There was no way that the fight venue could be kept secret – and once the magistrates heard about it they had to act. The organisers quickly changed the venue for the fight. The contestants, and thousands of their fans, therefore travelled to nearby Stratford. By the following morning the magistrates had also banned the event from happening there – as anticipated. Everyone then travelled back to Warwick, to Stank Hill, which was just outside the town magistrates' jurisdiction. It was a clever move by the organisers which caught the magistrates by surprise and gave them no time in which to act. They stood little chance of stopping the event anyway: thousands of bloodthirsty spectators were by now arriving in a steady stream. Any attempt to try and stop the contest would result in bloodshed.

THE FIGHT

Official reports for the day describe it as being dreadfully hot, with a temperature of 90 degrees Fahrenheit in the shade. In eager anticipation the crowd awaited the arrival of Tom Cannon and Jem Ward. Plenty of money had already changed hands as bets were placed on its outcome. No seats were provided, so the spectators watched the contest from whatever vantage point they could find. Most had to stand, but the wealthier spectators used their own private coaches.

The contestants came up to the scratch mark, and the crowd roared its approval as the fight began. There was no set time for the rounds, which only finished when a fighter was knocked to the ground.

From there he had to get back to the scratch line or be counted out. He was allowed thirty seconds to do so, plus a further eight in which to rest. Any contestant who drew blood got a rousing cheer. The contest would continue until one of the men had been knocked unconscious, or the fight was stopped.

Although he was the reigning champion, Tom Cannon was defeated in the tenth round. The whole contest lasted just ten minutes.

The second contest of the day was between Dick Curtis and Peter Warren. Whilst the contestants got ready, debts were settled between the punters from the first contest. Now it was time for various other dubious entrepreneurs to move in, to make their own killings amongst a crowd of very hot and thirsty spectators. For instance, oranges cost one shilling each (approximately £2.25 today); bottles of porter sold for five shillings and six shillings per bottle (approximately £11-£12 today). Yet these grossly inflated prices paled into insignificance when quarts of water were sold for seven shillings and sixpence (approximately £17 today)! Inevitably pick-pockets were at work amongst the crowd. So were other tricksters, who were only too happy to take money from the punters: their capers would have included dice throwing and 'thimble rigging' (the shell game). They firmly believed in the philosophy that a fool and his money are easily parted. And they were!

Dick Curtis, also known as the Pet of the Fancy, beat his opponent in the seventh round after just thirteen minutes. Nonetheless, it had been a good, albeit short, day's sport for the audience. No doubt they were happy to get out of the sweltering heat too. Many made their way home, but others returned to Warwick where they spent their money. Undoubtedly many of them would have heard about the different fights coming up within the next few days, and may have decided to stay in town.

The results of the two fights were printed later that evening in the *Globe* newspaper, 92 miles away in London.

ANOTHER WARWICK BOXER

Randolph Adolphus Turpin, also known as the Leamington Licker, is remembered in Warwick. In fact, his statue is the only piece of public statuary in the town. Whilst he was born in neighbouring Royal Leamington Spa, Randy (as he is affectionately known) spent some of his life in Warwick. He is best remembered for his amazing victory over Sugar Ray Robinson in July 1951. This victory made him the World Middleweight Champion, although it was a short reign.

Randy retired in 1962 after seventy-five professional bouts, sixty-six of which he won (forty-eight by knockout).

Sadly he fell into financial difficulties. He reportedly took his own life in 1966, after being made bankrupt. However, there is a school of thought that believes his death was not self-inflicted. The possibility remains that he was murdered.

Randolph Turpin. (Author's collection)

A carrier pigeon had taken just three hours to get there with the news.

Just a few days after the Cannon/Ward fight, approximately 800 bloodthirsty individuals calling themselves sportsmen flocked to Warwick and paid considerable sums of money to witness fighting bouts between two 'kings of the jungle' and several of man's best friends – lions versus dogs. In the middle of the Factory Yard, which measured 180ft x 100ft, stood a cage of 16ft x 10ft x 13ft. It was enclosed by metal bars, each one of which was about 9 inches apart. This was the venue for lions, provided by George Wombwell. The 'kings of the jungle' would be attacked in separate bouts by three fighting dogs at a time.

The organisers received more than £400 (approximately £18,000 today)

blood money from the admission fees alone. They claimed this amount was needed to host the event, and make good any damage that might be caused. This figure does not include the vast sums of money changing hands in bets.

An expectant hush greeted Wallace, who was the first lion, when he was put into the cage. Moments later his opponents, Captain, Turk and Tiger, were added and the contest began. The spectators shouted encouragement to the animals, and the roars and barks of the contestants added to the hideous uproar.

Captain lasted just six minutes before he was too badly mauled to continue. Bleeding heavily, he was removed to the cheering and booing of the spectators. His departure led to a stand-off between Wallace and the remaining dogs.

Wallace. (With permission of Saffron Walden museum)

Tiger had now lost any enthusiasm to rejoin the fray. But spurred on by the jeering crowds, plus threats and cajoling from his master, he attacked Wallace again. He was ably supported by Turk who was described as a game little fighter.

Nevertheless, it was all over within five minutes.

Clearly dying, Turk was removed. With all his support gone, Tiger lost what little remained of his waning enthusiasm, and Wallace was left the undoubted winner.

Poor Turk was not buried: his owner had his body stuffed, as a long-term memento of this barbaric event.

Whilst the cage was being prepared for the next contest, a surge of gatecrashers invaded the yard. They had jibbed at paying the admission fees of between one and two guineas (£45-£90 today), but were determined to enjoy the despicable entertainment all the same. Consequently, the start of the next fight was delayed – and what a different bout it proved to be!

Nero, a mild-tempered beast, was the second lion brought in to fight.

It was later revealed that Mr Wombwell had, rather foolishly, laid out 200 guineas (appoximately £9,000 today) on Nero winning this contest.

But, much to his owner's dismay, the lion had other ideas.

Nero was just not in a fighting mood, and he ignored the next three dogs when they were put into his cage. However, they did not ignore him, and quickly pinned him down. There was an absolute uproar in the crowd from Nero's backers, who hissed and jeered. Needless to say, the jubilant punters who had backed the dogs to win were ecstatic, and their owners claimed victory. Mr Wombwell objected to the result, and insisted another attempt should be made to make Nero fight. But Nero still refused to play. A third attempt followed, which also failed. Much to the glee of the dog supporters, Mr Wombwell accepted defeat.

ROUND TWO

Four days later there was a repeat performance in the Factory Yard, still without any hindrance from the magistrates. Why did they not act? Were they in the audience?

Having learned his lesson, Mr Wombwell only brought Wallace to this event, whilst he was still fresh from his previous victory. For this contest he would fight two dogs at a time on three occasions.

Admission was much cheaper, which no doubt encouraged a return visit from many of the brave sportsmen who had been at the earlier contests.

The first fight was no contest. Ball and Tinker, the chosen dogs, had no stomach for taking on Wallace. Conscious of the crowd's anger, their owners wasted no time in forcing the dogs into the cage.

NERO'S REVENGE

—⊗∞⊗—

Like elephants, lions never forget.

About three weeks later Nero was in his cage at Oxford Races. As it happened, one of the dog owners from the Warwick event stood too close to the cage. Recognising him, Nero attacked the man and ripped his coat!

—⊗∞⊗—

Wallace made short work of them, adding Tinker's subsequent death to his tally.

In the second contest Turpin showed a good deal of common sense: he ran away. Sweep was badly mauled, although he lived to fight another day. Wallace's backers were delighted.

For the dog backers, their remaining hopes depended on Tiger and Billy. But their luck continued on a downward spiral. Totally fired up, Wallace was in no mood to play and he made short shrift of them.

Tiger did not live up to his name, and like Turpin he was not stupid. Without stopping to fight, he ran – leaving Billy on his own. It was a wise decision.

Just a few minutes later, the hideously mauled Billy was removed. He died soon afterwards.

For the punters who had come for some spectacular entertainment, it had been a disappointment. Those who had backed Wallace went away to celebrate, leaving the losers to drown their sorrows.

THE AMAZING WALLACE

Wallace was born in Edinburgh in 1812, and has the distinction of being the first African lion to be born in captivity. It is thought he was named after William Wallace, the great Scottish freedom fighter.

Unlike Nero, Wallace was not such a mild-mannered beast. On one occasion, in the Leeds area, he attacked a man who had stupidly put his arm into the animal's cage. The man ultimately died of his injuries.

When Wallace died in 1838, his body was conveyed by stagecoach to Saffron Walden, near where George Wombwell was born. The lion's body was stuffed and donated to Saffron Walden museum, where he can be seen today.

It is highly likely that Wallace was the inspiration for the monologue of the Lion and Albert.

George Wombwell is buried in Highgate Cemetery, underneath a statue of Nero, who was his favourite. The lion is rumoured to have slept at the foot of his bed.

AD 1827/8

ARSON!

AFTER WHAT SEEMED like an eternity, the firemen arrived at Mrs Blick's farm, situated at Longbridge, on the outskirts of Warwick. They needed no directing: the flames, which were devouring the hayricks, lit up the night sky. It was obvious the firemen would need all the help they could get.

But it was not forthcoming.

There was no need to summon the farm workers and families from their beds: they were already awake, milling around – and doing nothing. In spite of being aware of the dangers of leaving a fire to burn unchecked, they showed a marked reluctance to actually start fighting the flames. None of the firemen lived in Longbridge, and they did not know where the water supply was.

'Where's the water?' they shouted.

Their questions were ignored.

Even when they approached individuals, the usual answers were 'don't know' or a nonchalant shrug of the shoulders. Neither threats nor cajoling had any effect on the unhelpful watchers.

Meanwhile, the more reliable employees and neighbours were fighting the blaze on their own. They bemoaned the lack of assistance from the fire brigade, unaware that they could not find any water.

It never occurred to the firemen to ask these people where they were getting their water. The firemen would later be severely criticised about their actions that night.

When water was finally found, it highlighted another problem: the fire hose had been burned, either deliberately or by accident, which caused further delays.

Fortunately more responsible people arrived and they helped to bring the fire under control – but not before a considerable amount of damage had been done to the affected ricks.

Why had the fires been started? Was it a grudge against just one rick owner which had spread? Or was it a grudge against the wealthier farmers in general? These questions were never answered. England was not a happy country in the early nineteenth century. Whilst the Industrial and Agricultural Revolutions brought prosperity to some, they caused untold misery for countless others. Following the defeat of Napoleon in 1815, England sank into an industrial and agricultural recession, and

THE CHURCH STREET HORROR!

Church Street, home of the Birmingham Fire Office, was the scene of a terrible accident in this era. On 10 January 1822, as a coach was travelling down Church Street, a young man called William Leeson, unbeknown to the guard, tried to climb onto its rear as a fare-dodging passenger. Unfortunately he missed his footing and fell under the wheels of the coach. He died the next morning.

The inquest was held on 14 January, and a verdict of accidental death was recorded. Both the coachman and guard were cleared of any blame.

Immediately after the inquest, an unnamed man tried what Leeson had attempted. He too fell under the wheels, though luckily he only suffered a fractured leg. He turned out to be one of the jurors who had sat on Leeson's inquest. Some people never learn.

outbreaks of violence were becoming common. The attitude of the farm labourers who had hindered the firemen showed that the local workers clearly had some grievances – but whether they were aimed at any specific person was never discovered.

Mr Hudson, from the Swan Hotel, lost wheat and hay to the value of £170 (approximately £8,000 today). His ricks were still burning the next day. Another man lost slightly less. Mrs Blick, the widowed owner of the farm, lost hay to the value of £200 (approximately £9,500 today). Luckily she was insured.

Bearing in mind the attitude of the unhelpful labourers, plus the current state of unrest in the countryside, arson was immediately suspected. The County Fire Office, who had insured Mrs Blick, offered a reward of £100 (approximately £4,700 today) for information leading to the arrest and prosecution of the offenders. In the event of there being more than one offender, a further offer was made to allow a felon to turn King's Evidence and testify against his co-defendants, thereby escaping prosecution. Some people will always turn a disaster to their advantage, and the Birmingham Fire Office, situated in Church Street, Warwick, was one such example. Within hours of the blaze it had promoted policies to insure against ricks being burnt: they cost a princely sum of one shilling and sixpence (approximately £3.75 today). Their directors also offered to link up with other fire offices to provide a more effective fire service for the town. They warned that the great fire of 1694 could happen again.

There was a sharp reminder that the problem had not really gone away four days later, when there was another arson attack on local ricks at Welford-on-Avon. Another fire followed in January.

ANONYMOUS LETTERS

On 8 January 1828, an anonymous letter addressed to Mr Perkins at nearby Leek Wootton was found in the Coventry Road, a little way outside Warwick. It read:

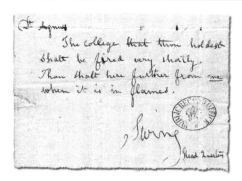

Example of a Swing letter.

Mr Perkins, sir,
Your ricks will be on fire tonight.

Two days later, the following letter was received at a house in Warwick Square:

I give you all notice that I am coming round to Warwick, when I shall make my visit to Mr Loveday's house, and then to the Chron [icle] office, and then I shall cut among the farmers, for I am determined to see the poor people no longer abused: Though I set the rick at Longbridge on fire, I did not think of setting fire to the barns of Mrs Blick, as she is a good widow.
I remain Mr Spindleshank's good servant
Mr Firelighter
Warwick January 10th
No jesting: I shall not fail in my attempt.

It did not happen.

FEARS IN THE COUNTRYSIDE

In Warwickshire and elsewhere, the newly developed agricultural

machinery resulted in the need for less workers and greater wealth for the farmers – but at a tremendous cost to the working class. Less work meant less money, less food and a growing resentment of the ruling classes. Much of the scarce agricultural employment was now offered only on a casual basis. Even the Poor Relief was reduced. These new practices led to unrest in the normally placid rural communities. Making matters worse, a huge post-war influx of discharged soldiers and sailors returned to the area, all seeking work. They swamped the labour markets.

Rick fires were one way for the disgruntled populace to give vent to their anger. The government knew what was happening, and likened it to France immediately before the Revolution. It dealt with public disorder quite ruthlessly. Matters came to a head in 1830 with the outbreak of the Swing Riots, directed against wealthy farmers. 'Captain Swing' did not actually exist: it was just a name adopted by the rioters. Whilst Warwickshire was not affected by the riots, the burning of ricks was not an isolated occurrence. No doubt, given

Typical agricultural machinery of the period.

time, the riots would have spread all over the country. The Swing Riots were aimed specifically at the tithes system operated by the Church, rich farmers and Poor Law Guardians. These people made the law harsher, and made it even more difficult to obtain relief.

Agricultural unrest had been fermenting for several years, but never on such a large scale. Damaging property was the primary object of the rioters, who were mainly agricultural labourers. No deaths happened until the authorities took their revenge. Ultimately, 19 rioters were hanged, 505 transported for life, 644 imprisoned, 7 fined, 1 whipped and 806 bound over to keep the peace.

ELECTION RIOTS

Earl Loses Control – But Not For Long!

THE VERY ANTI-CATHOLIC Henry Richard Greville, 3rd Earl of Warwick, was a borough recorder for Warwick, and lord lieutenant of the county. For generations his family, in common with most of his contemporaries, had exercised an undue influence on Warwick when it came to politics, both local and national. In 1831 there was no voting by secret ballot: votes were carried out by a show of hands. It was a risky business to go against the lord of the manor's wishes unless you were particularly powerful in your own right.

At general elections the lord of the manor decided who went into Parliament, and then ensured that it happened. Any opponents were quickly shown the error of their ways. Similar tactics could be used locally when electing a mayor. The system was a relic from medieval times when the lord of the manor was king in all but name.

This was the situation in Warwick during the run-up to the general election of 1831.

DIRTY TRICKS AND MORE DIRTY TRICKS

The earl's man was opposed by two candidates (whom he tried, unsuccessfully, to disqualify because they lived out of the area). Thirty-three inns had drinking accounts opened for the sole purpose of influencing his supporters. Not all of them were voters, but they helped in other ways. However, these dirty tricks angered the opposition, and the castle had to provide escorts for its supporters. It was typical of the corruption existing at the time, and highlighted the need for parliamentary reform.

In spite of all his efforts, the earl's man was not elected. But it was not the end of the story. Following the enactment of the Representation of the People Act in 1832, there was another general election later in the year. This was even more controversial than the previous one had been, as the new legislation did nothing to prevent voters being bribed. It was a loophole the earl had every intention of exploiting – although he later denied doing so, blaming his agents.

Market Place. (Author's collection)

In August Charles Greville, the earl's man, hosted a grand dinner in Warwick Market Place, which was attended by 2,500 of his supporters (not all of whom would have been able to vote). Afterwards he set up his headquarters at the Black Horse. In total he spent approximately £10,000 (in today's money) treating his supporters – or to be more accurate, he spent £10,000 of the earl's money, albeit in their mutual cause. Suddenly some of the electoral boundaries on the Castle Estate were moved, and new lodgers were leased properties at a very preferential rate – provided that they voted for Charles Greville.

The castle's supporters paraded regularly around the town. They were protected by clubmen, who were paid five shillings a day (approximately £12 today). Their purpose was to intimidate the opposition. Regardless of the change in the law, the earl was determined his man would win. Whilst the opposition adopted similar tactics, they did not have the financial resources enjoyed by the earl. Following the passing of the Act, there was also considerable apathy amongst the voters.

TROOPS ON THE STREETS

Nevertheless, in the days immediately before the election there were riots. These caused considerable damage, and several people were injured. There were, as yet, no policemen in Warwick, so the magistrates called for military assistance to restore order in the town. This was provided by the Scots Greys who just happened to be in the area. They were a long-established regiment of dragoons, well experienced in all manner of fighting. Since gaining immortal fame in 1815 at the Battle of Waterloo, they had become very experienced in policing and quelling riots. On their large horses, they made very formidable opponents. Very few rioters were prepared to face them, and peace was quickly restored – but not for long. Voting had to be suspended

THE GREAT REFORM ACT (1832)

The Great Reform Act (or, to use its proper name, the Representation of the People Act) was passed on 4 June 1832, and received royal assent a few days later. Now the vote was extended to 650,000 people (it was previously 400,000). In reality, whilst extending the vote to one in six adult males, this did nothing for the poor. They still had no vote. Men aged twenty-one years or older did not get the vote until 1867; women were not given similar rights until 1928.

following further rioting when election booths were overturned.

No one was really surprised when Charles Greville won.

WITNESSES NOBBLED

But if he thought his seat in Parliament was secure, he was in for a major shock. His opponents made an official complaint about the way the campaign had been handled, citing the underhand and very questionable methods employed by the earl. A full investigation exonerated Charles Greville, although it was agreed that there had been an extensive use of bribery and corruption by his supporters. Many accusing fingers were pointed at the earl. To his credit, Charles resigned his seat.

The subsequent enquiry concentrated on the devious way the borough boundaries had been changed just before the election. Clearly this had all been part of the earl's tactics, especially as these changes had since been incorporated into neighbouring Leamington. As expected, the earl steadfastly denied the allegations. He blamed his agents for exceeding their authority. Matters came to a head in May 1834 when a writ for bribery and corruption was served. But any joy his enemies might have felt soon evaporated: when it came to calling witnesses to testify against him, the court found that they were much too terrified to appear. Undoubtedly they had been 'nobbled'. It was never established just how far the earl was involved. Suffice to say that the whole affair quietly died away.

AD 1849

CHOLERA STRIKES!

WARWICK IS A hill town, and drainage should have been easy. However, it was definitely a problem, with dreadful consequences: in 1849 there was an outbreak of Asiatic cholera in Warwick.

This disease is an infection of the small intestine caused by the bacterium *Vibrio cholera*. Its main characteristics are watery diarrhoea and a flow of bile. It is rarely passed from person to person, being contracted by consuming contaminated water. In Victorian England, stomach complaints and bowel disorders of all sorts were accepted as a part of everyday life. As the century progressed, however, this attitude changed. Death and disease could no longer be conveniently limited to the poor and needy: they affected everybody. In 1849 Warwick was an unhealthy place to live, with a high rate of bowel disorders.

Earlier that year a damning report was published regarding the sanitation – or rather lack of it – which existed in Warwick. The report highlighted a scandalous and embarrassing situation, and it concentrated on the general and accepted unhealthy practices in many parts of the town. It also highlighted over 400 specific nuisances in the town, including fifty-nine cesspools, seventy-one open privies, sixty-four 'filthy houses' and forty-nine offensive drains.

Between 1847 and 1849 the mortality rate in Warwick had risen dramatically,

Cholera strikes! (LC-USZC4-9858)

Cleaning the streets of Warwick. (Author's collection)

with overcrowding to blame for most of it. One area, Woodward Court, consisted of six houses in which 200 people lived. Beggars who came for the races and the fairs had pushed the numbers up dramatically. Brookhouse Buildings housed 200-300 inhabitants and provided two pigsties, two pumps and two privies. These courts were generally considered to be close, dirty, undrained, damp and very filthy. The stench of human sewage would have been horrendous. The medical men of the day blamed these 'exhalations' for causing the disease: only later would they discover the real cause. Imagine the reports we receive today on the insanitary state of poor countries elsewhere in the world, and think: this is what Warwick would have been like 150 years ago!

When coupled with an inadequate and often unhealthy supply of drinking water, the town became a wonderful breeding ground for a local outbreak of Asiatic cholera. For instance, the water

from the ditch in St John's Meadow contained raw sewage and was a wonderful source of fever. Water from Priory Pools and the Avon was described as being 'very hard and impure'. The obvious answer was to do something about creating a proper supply of fresh water. Various plans were put forward, but only one was accepted: this was situated at Portobello and cost £15,000 (approximately £760,000 today). Whilst it increased the supply of water to the town, the supply was of a poor quality, and the water was often polluted by raw sewage from Kenilworth and Coventry.

Once the disease was recognised, members of the Local Board of Health and the Board Guardians had to take action. But there were those who were more concerned about the cost than the desperate need for action. The groups also lacked any co-ordination in the way they worked. There were six inspectors to examine the various nuisances in the town, but they rarely spoke to each other. Although a pump situated near

OTHER PUBLIC NUISANCES IN WARWICK

∽

Long before this outbreak of cholera (and afterwards too) there were complaints about the unhealthy state of the town. These are just a few examples:

1610: Dung being left in Foxes Lane (now Back Lane).
1611: a) Geese and ducks allowed to swim in Joyce Pool, which was a source of drinking water. b) Swine roaming loose in the churchyard, and pig troughs erected on the highway.
1648: A scavenger was appointed to clear the four main streets around the Market Place.
1827: Privies to be emptied before 9 a.m. in the summer and 10 a.m. in the winter.
1857: A lack of urinals.
1884: Urinals by the Museum not being used. (This begs the question of what was being used instead…)
1885: Objectionable exhibitions at fairs (no details shown).
1891: Stench in the Market Place.
1895: Increase in dogs running loose.
1904: People cycling on the footpaths.
1905: Noise from electric trams when on a curve.

∽

a leaking dung heap was not used for supplying drinking water, it still supplied washing purposes including crockery and laundry, and was not considered to be a health risk until later.

TREATING THE SICK

The obvious course of action was to isolate the infected people – easier said than done. Owners of suitable properties refused to allow them to be used for such purposes. It was a wonderful display of nimbyism (not in my back yard).

Hysteria and ill-feelings towards the sufferers quickly spread, and no workman would disinfect and lime-wash the houses belonging to the cholera victims. Modern research suggests that using chloride of lime would have been of little use. Fires were lit in the streets in an effort to purify the air. Pepper Alley, situated by the side of the Antelope Inn, was one of the worst areas affected areas. The actual number of fatalities in the town is not recorded. Before this pandemic had run its course the real cause of cholera had been established, so local doctors knew that drinking contaminated water was the cause, rather than inhaling smelly air. William Lambe was way ahead of his time.

AD 1860

GET THE HANGMAN!

'It's Throttler! Get him!'

Just when George Smith, hangman from the Black Country, thought his day could not get any worse, it did. This whole affair had been an absolute disaster from start to finish. Although he was only partly to blame, it soon became a hanging he wished he could forget.

This story began in Birmingham when a young but jealous and suspicious Irishman called Francis Price fell in love with a servant girl. Sadly she did not feel the same way about him. Believing she was having an affair with a Birmingham city policeman, he decided to confront her. They had an argument, during which he fatally stabbed her. He was then chased into a nearby Anglican church where he hoped to claim sanctuary (although he was a Roman Catholic by faith). His pursuers were not deterred, and Price was quickly arrested.

He appeared at Warwick Assizes, which was where serious crimes committed in Birmingham were tried. No one was surprised when he was found guilty and sentenced to death.

EXECUTION DELAYED

Throttler, as Smith was commonly known, happily agreed to carry out the execution, and until the actual day everything had gone according to plan.

But then it all went wrong.

Being the year 1860, there were less and less public executions taking place, and this one was not going to be missed. Who knew when the next one might be? There was also a growing acceptance that public executions would soon become a thing of the past, so this might possibly be the last chance many people had to witness one.

Price's execution was fixed for 8 a.m. on a Friday, which was the traditional time. During the previous day and night, hordes of ghoulish spectators descended on the town, determined not to miss the fun.

Long before 8 a.m. they were in place, but as the execution warrant did not arrive the hanging was postponed until the next day. Although it was not Throttler's fault, he was blamed. Having nothing else to do but wait, the crowds visited the town's inns and generally enjoyed themselves. During the day

Scene at a typical Victorian hanging.

more spectators arrived. They joined the others on the Saturday morning outside the prison, jostling and bartering for the best positions.

But the execution warrant still did not arrive.

Executions could not take place on the Sabbath, so the ghouls had to endure another day of enforced idleness, impatience and alcohol. At last Monday morning arrived – and so did the execution warrant.

It was the moment they had been waiting for, and time for the next problem.

UNHAPPY CROWDS

In 1860 the gaol was moved from the town centre. Its new position was out at the area known as the Cape. It was a brand-new prison but, as the crowds now discovered, viewing was limited when it came to executions. Only one third of the crowd could see anything! Already in a bad mood because of all the waiting, and now suffering from restricted viewing, the mob were most unhappy. Whilst none of these issues had been Throttler's fault, that was all about to change. Throttler opened the trapdoor before his victim had finished praying – something that just was not done. For the angry crowds, it was the last straw.

'Kill the hangman!' came the cry.

Only too aware of the crowd's growing animosity, Throttler waited until the early afternoon before arriving at Warwick railway station to journey home. He should have waited a little longer. As he went out onto the platform Throttler was recognised. A mob of about 300 angry and cheated spectators surged towards him: they needed a target for their anger, and who better than the hangman?

'Put him on the rails and let the next train run him over!' shouted someone.

'Yes! Yes!' The cry was taken up by others.

Moments later they grabbed Throttler and pulled him onto the railway track. There was no shortage of hands to hold him there.

Quite clearly they intended to murder him.

'Look out!' shouted Mr Chilton, the station master, who had seen what was happening. 'There's a train coming!'

Suddenly the rioters' bravery vanished and they all clambered quickly back onto the platform. By the time they realised that there was no train, Mr Chilton had taken Throttler to the other platform and locked him in the second-class waiting room. Only when the mob had gone did Mr Chilton release him.

GEORGE 'THROTTLER' SMITH

Well known on the Midlands execution circuit, George went by the nickname of 'Throttler' for obvious reasons connected with his trade. (Throttler was not his only nickname: the other one was 'Topper', referring to his habit of wearing a top hat whilst working.) His was a job very few people wanted, though they were quite happy to watch him carry it out – it was all part of a good day's entertainment.

When a hanging was over, Throttler cut up the rope into small pieces and sold them off as souvenirs. It is thought he coined the expression 'money for old rope'.

His main failing was drinking too much, a vice which, coupled with dropsy, ultimately killed him.

He had become a hangman by chance. There was an execution due at the prison in which he was held, and when the hangman arrived there was no assistant to help him. The prison governor offered a pardon to anyone who would assist – and Throttler accepted the offer.

His last execution at Stafford, in 1866, was a disaster. The rope slipped, and the condemned man fell to the ground. It took another six minutes for him to retie the rope and do the job properly.

He never officiated at a hanging again.

AD 1868

FENIAN TRIAL FEARS

'**T**HE FENIANS ARE** coming to Warwick!'

In 1868, with Fenian fears at fever pitch in London, these were the last words the local police and prison authorities wanted to hear. Why were Fenians coming here? On 9 January 1868 any hopes of it being a mistake were dashed when Warwick Gaol received two Fenian prisoners. The governor of the gaol, and the police, would have been much happier if they had stayed in London.

One of them, Ricard (no h) O'Sullivan Burke, captured in London, had a very bad reputation. The other prisoner, Joseph Casey, was arrested for trying to help him escape. After their initial arrest, Burke and Casey had been incarcerated in the Clerkenwell House of Detention in London. Burke's capture was a severe blow to the Fenians, and plans were soon underway to rescue him. Although the police knew what was being planned, they believed that any rescue attempt would be made by tunnelling under the prison walls. Consequently – and unbelievably – the patrolling police ignored a barrel which was placed beside the wall. It never occurred to anyone

that the barrel might have contained gunpowder – but it did!

Luckily it failed to ignite, and the ruse was discovered.

In spite of such a lucky escape, the police still believed a tunnel would be used, and they did not change their plans. Even more inexplicably, they also ignored a second barrel placed in the same place the next day. This time the barrel, again filled with gunpowder, exploded: twelve people were killed, and many more were injured. The explosion also caused a backlash against the local Irish community. Not trusting the police, the governor made his own plans and had previously moved Burke and Casey to another part of the prison. This prevented their escape. But London was now in a state of panic – where would the next outrage occur? It was obvious that Sir Richard Mayne, the seventy-one-year-old Commissioner of the Metropolitan Police, had failed to take the rescue warnings seriously. The authorities feared another rescue attempt, and arrived at a novel way of dealing with this particular problem. (Mayne was excluded from their planning.) The police realised that

Warwick Gaol. (Author's collection)

Burke was also wanted in Birmingham for buying firearms. So, when the two men appeared at Bow Street Court on 9 January 1868 it was quickly agreed that they should be sent up to Warwick to stand trial at the next assizes. It was for this reason that the Fenians arrived in Warwick.

Later that same evening they arrived at Warwick Gaol with an escort of two superintendents, a detective and sixteen constables (all armed with cutlasses and revolvers). The London officers handed over their charges and relaxed. The prison staff had no such luck. Their problems were only just beginning. On arrival the prisoners were put into solitary confinement, and guarded, day and night, by armed warders. After some discussion, the lord lieutenant of Warwickshire applied to the Home Secretary for military assistance. Such action is only ever taken in exceptional circumstances, when the civil powers cannot cope, and it is not a course of action to be undertaken lightly. In reply, Captain Heath offered the services of the local volunteers to help guard the prisoners, day and night, and so to prevent any escapes. His offer was gratefully accepted, and the men were sworn in as special constables. This gave them police powers. They continued with this duty until relieved by Captain Norris and two companies of the Rifle Brigade from Weedon. A worried police and prison staff, as well as the local residents, heaved a big sigh of relief when they arrived.

The county authorities still had a major problem on their hands, though. The next assizes, where the men would be tried, were fast approaching, and there was every chance that they would receive long

THE FENIANS

Fenians took their name from the mythical Fianna warrior bands in Ireland who could be called upon in times of trouble. The term was first used to describe Irish Republican groups in North America in 1858. They were guided by the principles that Ireland had a natural right to independence which could only be won through armed rebellion. Today the term 'Fenian' tends to be used mostly in Northern Ireland. It is now a derogatory term used to describe Roman Catholics; Irish Nationals prefer to be called Nationalists or Republicans.

sentences. If so the problem would stay in Warwick for years to come. Extra guards would be needed, at an exceptionally high cost. Something had to be done.

The legal minds got together and came up with a plan. They applied to the Queen's Bench Division to have both the prisoners returned to London for their trial. It was argued that as most of the witnesses lived in London it would be to everyone's benefit to move the trial back to the capital. On 6 March, Burke and Casey were returned to London for their trial. The Rifle Brigade returned to its barracks, and the police gratefully hung up their cutlasses and revolvers.

Burke was sentenced to fourteen years' imprisonment. He was never the same after his release. Casey was acquitted of obstructing Burke's arrest.

AD 1887-1889

BENT BANKERS
BANGED UP

'**H**AVE YOU HEARD? Greenways have gone bust!' The news spread around Warwick and elsewhere like a bush fire. It sounded unbelievable, but nevertheless it was true.

The long-established Greenway, Smith and Greenway Bank had gone into receivership, causing heavy financial losses to its clients.

At first the two senior partners received plenty of sympathy, as they now faced personal bankruptcy proceedings. But it did not last long. Whilst they always portrayed themselves as being innocent victims of the collapse, they soon revealed a total disdain for their creditors.

Kelynge Greenway lived in Jury Street, in what is now called Pageant House. He had been a well-respected man from a long-standing Warwick

Warwickshire banknote. (Author's collection)

family, and had married into money. His brother, George, was the other partner. George was a highly regarded solicitor, and the Warwick town clerk. George's last known honourable act was to resign from that position as the brothers became embroiled in a bitter quarrel with their creditors. Had they acted in a more contrite fashion then the outcome of the whole affair might have been different.

Irrespective of the bank's collapse, the pair continued to enjoy a life of luxury, and openly defied their creditors. To really rub salt into the wound they employed the country's leading lawyers to find ways for them to avoid their responsibilities. Their lifestyle intrigued the official receiver, Thomas Peirson, who was looking into their personal financial affairs. He was empowered to do so by the Bankruptcy Act of 1883. As his enquiries progressed, he unearthed some interesting facts about the brothers. Both men had extensive personal overdrafts at their own bank, and clearly lived off their creditors. There was plenty of this type of evidence, but it was not enough to build a criminal case against them. He needed much more direct evidence of fraud. He hoped his luck had changed in 1888 when Richard Walsh, a farm labourer, threatened to kill Kelynge Greenway: when Walsh appeared in court he was treated leniently because he had lost money when the bank collapsed. Surprisingly no other people came forward to complain, and Peirson began to struggle. He was coming under pressure from the creditors to get their money back. There was now little or no money to distribute. Whilst George's house was for sale, Kelynge's wife continued to support her husband's extravagant lifestyle with her own money – and there was nothing Peirson could do about it. The brothers obviously felt confident the whole affair would blow over. Then Peirson had a surprise visit from George Cable Lake, the former bank manager, who felt his loyalty to the brothers had now ended. And he had an interesting tale to tell about Frederick Cooper's bill of exchange...

Pageant House. (Author's collection)

THE BANK MANAGER'S TALE

In the mid-1870s Frederick returned from Australia and settled in Warwick. He regularly received bills of exchange from his investments. These he paid into Greenways for onward transmission to Glynn's Bank in London. When they were redeemed, the money was credited to his account in Warwick. On 15 August 1887 Frederick paid in a bill of exchange for £1,200 (approximately £67,000 today). It was not ready for payment, and when Greenways collapsed the following month he demanded the return of his bill. Whilst his letter was acknowledged, the bill was not returned. On 20 August, George Lake could show that Kelynge's personal overdraft was £3,943 (approximately £221,000 today) – and that it had just been reduced by £1,200. Kelynge had used Frederick's money to do it.

Peirson was delighted. He now had enough evidence to support a criminal charge against Kelynge. This information encouraged him to dig deeper into George's affairs – and it paid dividends! George Greenway had used a client's money, held in trust, to legitimately purchase shares. So far, so good, until he sold the shares, without informing the trust, and used the money in a futile attempt to try and prop up the failing bank.

The brothers pleaded not guilty to the charges at Warwick Assizes in July 1888. Admission to the limited space in the public gallery was by ticket only, and 90 per cent of the would-be spectators were turned away. Kelynge kept the court waiting – he was busy talking to friends. He was defended by Sir Charles

Russell, considered to be the best lawyer in the land, with a retaining fee of 500 guineas (approximately £30,000 today). Undoubtedly he was funded in this by his wife. It was another way of Kelynge showing contempt for his creditors. The jury returned guilty verdicts on the main charges. Thanks to Kelynge's lawyer, he was acquitted of being involved in the sale of the shares. George was sent to prison for five years, but Kelynge only received a twelve-month sentence (considered unduly lenient).

Warwick Station. (Author's collection)

But that is not the end of the story.

Kelynge served his sentence and was duly released. As he left the security of Warwick Gaol he was met by an angry mob. They frogmarched him to the railway station, determined to run him out of town. He was put into the last compartment on the first train for Birmingham, and warned never to return. The crowd then stayed on the platform and watched the train depart. But then it stopped, leaving Kelynge's compartment on the platform. The crowd soon gave way to hoots of laughter when they realised why the train had stopped: it was to enable a policeman to take a handcuffed prisoner back to Birmingham. And the only compartment they could use was the one in which Kelynge was seated...

THE PAGEANT HOUSE

Once inhabited by Kelynge Greenway, this Grade II listed building was used in connection with the 1906 Warwick Pageant. Here 300 ladies made 1,400 costumes and 40 artists painted the banners etc. that were needed. In total there were 2,000 performers in the pageant, directed by Louis Napoleon Parker. It was a condition of those taking part that they had to remain anonymous. Now known as the Pageant House, the building was bought for the town with the proceeds from the pageant. In 1974 it was taken over by Warwick District Council, and is still used for various activities.

AD 1892

AN EMBARRASSING CASE OF MURDER

'**WHO'S THERE?**' CALLED Private Bray.

Somehow he was not surprised when there was no immediate answer to his question: only more groaning, which came again from the direction of Priory Park.

Somebody was definitely in pain.

He stood irresolute for a few moments. What should he do?

He could easily walk away, as it was late and he should be on his way back to the barracks. Whatever was happening in the park was nothing to do with him. But curiosity, and possibly a twinge of conscience, made him want to investigate further. Nevertheless, he felt it could be risky on his own, so he went into the nearby police station and reported what he had heard. Several minutes later he took Police Sergeant Webb into Priory Park. There they found a man lying on the grass. Assuming he was drunk, they carried him back to the police station. Once in the light, Sergeant Webb realised the man had been badly beaten, especially about his head. By the time a doctor was summoned the injured man was dead. Police Inspector Stephen Hall began a murder enquiry.

The dead man was identified as James Russell, an inoffensive individual who lived with his wife and seven children in the Saltisford. Looking carefully at Russell's body, Stephen Hall was convinced the injuries had been caused by belt buckles. And he only knew of one particular group of men who used buckles in this way – soldiers.

There had been several disturbances with the military that evening, and it did not take him long to have the names of two suspects. They were Privates James Welch, a powerful former boxer from Birmingham, and Frederick Thomas King, a more slightly built man.

The police quickly went to the nearby barracks at Budbrooke and arrested them. King, in fact, had been confined to barracks on the evening of the murder, but had climbed over a wall and gone into town nonetheless. On his return, he was seen to have a lot of mud on his greatcoat.

Whilst Hall was certain he had the murderers in custody, he was only too aware he had very little evidence to support a prosecution. And there had been many soldiers in town that Saturday.

LACK OF EVIDENCE

During the afternoon there had been a football match at Emscote, which the military won. Celebrations moved into the Lord Nelson Inn, and started off very amicably. But it was here where trouble began.

Edith Russell, the dead man's sister, worked here as a barmaid. The customers had been good-humoured at first. Then an unidentified soldier made an offensive remark to Edith: James overheard it and took issue with the man, who in return challenged him to step outside. James refused, deciding that discretion was the better part of valour. Leaving the Lord Nelson, he moved to the Avon Tavern, which he left at about 10 p.m. Several witnesses testified that they thought they had seen James with

some soldiers. Other witnesses had seen a man and two soldiers going into Priory Park, but they were unable to positively identify any of them.

As Stephen Hall pieced his case together, he knew the evidence was not as strong as he would have liked.

When the scene was searched in daylight, a military cane and regimental greatcoat button were found. So was a silver ring of a sort which was regularly purchased by soldiers.

King's greatcoat was also covered in what appeared to be blood. However, being 1892, this could not be positively proved as such. As a bonus, King's overcoat had a button freshly sewn onto it. Whilst this thread was dry, the rest of the coat was wet. But the button found at the scene was not a Warwickshire Regimental one and, in spite of all the

CONSPIRACY THEORIES

PC William Hine. (Author's Collection)

Six years previously, in 1886, Police Constable William Hine of the Warwickshire Constabulary was murdered at Fenny Compton. When he failed to turn up for duty at Warwick Races, it was thought that he had absconded. He had made a late-night patrol of Fenny Compton, but was never seen alive again. Fenny Compton was searched, and his body was found in the canal. It was another embarrassing case for the Warwickshire Constabulary; in common with the James Russell case, no one was ever brought to justice.

It was suggested that James Russell knew the identity of his killers, and had been murdered to keep him quiet. There has never been any evidence to support this theory.

Police Headquarters. (Author's collection)

publicity, Hall could not find a single witness who had seen any soldiers and James Russell together. Even his sister maintained she could not remember any incident in the Lord Nelson which involved him. She thought there had been some sort of altercation, but knew nothing more than that.

When the magistrates committed the men for trial, the courtroom was packed with many spectators. It was described as being like an 'exotic conservatory' – less its purity and pleasantness of odour! In due course the two privates appeared at Warwick Assizes charged with murder. As was the practice, the case was outlined to the grand jury to decide whether there was enough evidence for trial. The grand jury decided that there was insufficient evidence, and the two men were acquitted.

It is always embarrassing for the police to lose a high-profile case. But what made this case even more embarrassing was the location of this crime: James Russell was murdered only a few yards away from the Constabulary Headquarters.

DARLING DAISY OUTWITTED BY THE PALACE

FRANCES EVELYN GREVILLE, *neé* Maynard, known as Darling Daisy and Babbling Brook, but in reality the Countess of Warwick, was furious. She had just visited a shop in Royal Leamington Spa and been told that the proprietor 'had nothing to interest her in his shop that day' – in other words, she would not get any more credit until she settled her account. For Daisy that was a real problem. She did not have any money.

Although there were all manner of treasures back home in Warwick Castle, they were not hers to sell. In any case, as her total debts were somewhere in the region of £100,000 (approximately £4,000,000 today) it is doubtful that their sale would have raised enough money. It is fair to say that Daisy never had a clue about money. She took it for granted that everyone was rich, and never had any qualms about spending.

For example, Daisy's parties were always much sought after in her upper-class social circle. One of her most talked-about events was a *bal poudré*, or powdered ball, which was held at the castle in 1895. It was an amazingly extravagant affair. Marie-Antoinette had always been one of Daisy's favourite characters, and this was very much reflected in the ball's theme: all the guests had to wear authentic late eighteenth-century French-style clothes, with matching hairstyles. Since Daisy was now well established as the latest

Daisy, Countess of Warwick. (Author's collection)

and most important mistress of Edward, Prince of Wales (later King Edward VII), she dressed as Marie-Antoinette. Her gown, along with most of her other dresses, came from the House of Worth, and each cost a minimum of £110 (approximately £5,600 today). She also wore a fur mantle costing £800 (approximately £45,300 today) – which she lost!

The problem she now faced was how best to solve her financial problems. And Daisy was very resourceful.

OUR LOVELY LITTLE DAISY WIFE

Daisy never lacked for male admirers and lovers. The Earl of Warwick seemed to accept the situation, common enough in the upper classes at the time. However, whilst sexual infidelity was acceptable, becoming emotionally involved was not.

So Daisy decided to use the compromising letters she had received from her royal lover to settle her debts. One of Edward's letters described her as 'our lovely little Daisy wife'. His numerous affairs had caused problems within the royal family before, and the last thing his son, George V, wanted was to have them raked up again. They would only embarrass his mother. Edward had died in 1910, so he could not be harmed if the letters were published – but Daisy reckoned on the royal family buying them from her to prevent their publication.

She used a friend, Arthur du Cros, as her agent. He was one of her creditors, so undoubtedly she did not tell him the whole story. As a back-up plan she also

had the American writer Frank Harris waiting in the side-lines in case her first plan failed – if the royal family did not buy the letters, she was quite prepared to publish them. James Thomas Harris (1856-1931) was born in Galway, and later became a naturalised American. He was always known as Frank. Described as an irascible and aggressive character, he tried his hand at all manner of jobs before obtaining a law degree. Unable to settle at practising law, he turned instead to writing. He is probably best remembered for his highly explicit novel *My Life and Loves*, which was banned in several countries. As the negotiations proceeded, Daisy announced that she had already sold her story to Harris and would let him use the letters to support it. She reasoned, quite correctly, that the palace would not let him have them to the detriment of George V's mother.

What Daisy failed to realise was that she was not the only one who could be devious.

The palace indicated that they would purchase the letters – and then they played for time. (Meanwhile, the Arch-Duke Franz Ferdinand and his wife very inconveniently got themselves

Edward VII and Queen Alexandra.

assassinated in Sarajevo, and Daisy's letters became less important as the world hurtled towards war.) Then the palace struck back. In a master-stroke, one which Daisy had not anticipated, the palace acquired a temporary injunction against her which forbade her disposing of the letters. In all her scheming she had overlooked one very important fact: whilst she might, physically, be in possession of the letters, their actual copyright belonged to Edward – and it had now passed to his son. In other words, the letters were not hers to sell. In theory she now had to surrender them – but that was not what Daisy planned. Undeterred by this setback, she announced that she would publish her memoirs – and that they would still include the details of her affair with Edward.

But she was too late.

The recently passed Defence of the Realm Act made an attack on any member of the royal family a treasonable offence. And publishing these letters would easily be construed as doing just that.

She had to shut up or be shut up.

With all her plans gone astray, Daisy turned to Arthur du Cros and pleaded for his help. He readily gave it, forgoing his own loan to her in the process, and helped her out of her difficulty.

Ironically the loss of her fur mantle at the *bal poudré* ultimately led to her becoming involved in politics. In 1923 she stood for Parliament as a socialist candidate against her daughter's step-daughter's husband: Anthony Eden.

She did not win.

True to her views on money, when Daisy died in 1938 she left over 500 birds from her collection, all to her long-suffering housekeeper. As these cost £8 a week (approximately £240 today) to feed, the poor woman had to get rid of most of them.

LIFE IN WARWICK DURING THE FIRST WORLD WAR

EXCEPT FOR THOSE who had menfolk serving in France, the war initially did not have too much of an impact on the town of Warwick. However, that began to change once the casualty notices started to appear in the local newspaper. They were also posted on the churchyard railings in Church Street. Promotions and medals awarded also began to appear in the local press. Life went on, but slowly the inhabitants of Warwick – along with the rest of the country – was forced to pay more attention to the war effort, both from an agricultural and industrial point of view. Once conscription was introduced, everything changed.

Coming into force on 2 March 1916, the Military Service Act required all single men between the ages of eighteen and forty-one to be conscripted into the Armed Services. Initially married men, or those widowed with children, were exempt. There were a few other exemptions too: ministers of religion, for example, and those men working in so-called 'reserved occupations'. The term 'reserved occupation' was difficult to define, and much depended on an individual's personal circumstances. Only too aware of the numerous anomalies that would be thrown up, Military Service Tribunals were set up to examine each application. One was based in Warwick, and was in frequent use. The tribunal had the power to approve full exemptions, or to apply conditions. Alternatively they could dismiss the application altogether.

By May 1916, married men were no longer exempt from conscription, and the maximum age of recruits was raised to fifty-one in 1918.

> Joseph Westley Stops was fined £25 – or fourteen days in prison in lieu – for failing to attend a hearing by the tribunal which aimed to examine whether he should be exempt from military service.

Runaway Tram

On 4 January 1916 conductress Elsie Hoskins released the brake of the No. 7 tram, waiting outside the Warwick Arms, just as she always did. It was only as the vehicle began to gather speed, rushing down Jury Street, she realised that the driver was not on board! But by then it was too late to stop, and the tram was totally out of control. As it entered the curve which went around Eastgate, the tram came off the rails and crashed into the front of the Castle Arms. All three passengers were injured, and considerable damage was done to the inn.

By early 1918 food rationing had been introduced, and supplies were short. Official pigeon-shooters were hired to combat the damage these birds were doing to crops. A shortage of meat meant that butchers closed for business on Mondays, Tuesdays and Wednesdays. When meat was rationed, cards would be sent through the post. The ration cards included offal, bones, rabbits and tinned meat. Advance warning of forthcoming rationing of tea, butter and margarine in early 1918 led to problems with panic buying: following a delivery of margarine to the Maypole Dairy in Smith Street, a queue of people in excess of 200 formed. Other food suppliers appeared to have very little or no deliveries. Consequently, the authorities seized 15 cwts of the margarine and redistributed it to other suppliers.

Later on, United Creameries of Wigtownshire were fined £100 (approximately £2,000 today) and £10 10s (approximately £210 today) costs for selling margarine at an illegally inflated price to Thacker & Christmas in Warwick. They were fined £10 (approximately £200 today) for passing that price on to their customers.

In 1918 fears were expressed that the lack of young men to act as farm hands was leading to a milk famine. Milk scams became common. For example,

The tram crash in 1916. (Author's collection)

MOTOR FUEL LEGISLATION INFRINGEMENTS

Brigadier General E.A. Grove was summoned for infringing the motor-fuel legislation (though full details of the offence were not disclosed). However, the summons was then withdrawn, on instructions from the deputy chief constable, as he could only be dealt with by the military!

There does not appear to be any record of what happened to him – unlike ordinary, non-military personnel in senior ranks, who were fined.

---

dairyman Philip Hirkin from Smith Street was fined £26 (approximately £520 today) and £1 (approximately £20 today) costs for diluting milk and 'selling it to the prejudice of the purchaser'. It was his second offence.

Funds were collected for providing food parcels for British prisoners of war in Germany. For a long time people back in England had been completely unaware of the food shortages being experienced by prisoners. One prisoner, Frank Warner, from Guy Street, send a coded message back home highlighting their plight. Whenever food was delivered, the prisoners had to fight for it. If they tried to take more, they would be hit by their guards. Frank described it as 'a terrible time'. He managed to bypass the censors at the prison by signing his letter home with the name 'W.E.R Starving'. His letter resulted in food parcels being sent to the prisoners. The same generosity was not extended to German prisoners. Arthur White, baker, was fined £40 (approximately £800 today) and his companion Robert Shellard, a card seller, £5 (approximately £100 today) by Warwick magistrate after they sold some bread to German prisoners of war who stated they were hungry. Their generous act was considered to a very serious matter, as it interfered with the administration of discipline in a nearby camp. In fact they were lucky: in the North Warwickshire town of Atherstone, at the same time, an eighteen-year-old girl was sent to prison for one month for a similar offence.

Frank was moved to Switzerland and repatriated in late June 1918. Following the end of the war, prisoners began returning in late November. They claimed they had survived captivity because 'the one thing the Germans could never understand about us was that we would laugh and would keep our spirits up somehow.'

BIG GUN WEEK

This event was scheduled to run between 11-16 November 1918, with the aim of raising £60,000 (approximately £1,200,000 today) investment in War Bonds; £15,000 (approximately £300,000 today) had already been promised.

On 9 November it had been reported that 'the end of the war was nigh', and expectations were high. People came into the town from the country, especially

KAISER HANGED IN WARWICK

⟶ ∞∞∞ ⟵

As the morning progressed, ropes were strung across High Street. When all was ready a straw effigy, easily recognisable as Kaiser Wilhelm II, was hanged from them, to a suitable roar of approval from the throngs of happy people. The real kaiser died in exile in the Netherlands on 3 June 1941, shortly before the Nazis invaded that country.

⟶ ∞∞∞ ⟵

Kaiser Wilhelm with Winston Churchill as a young man. (Library of Congress, LC-USZ62-75524)

those with relatives who were fighting or prisoners, to see if the rumours were true. Soon after 11 a.m. on Monday, 11 November 1918 a telegram appeared in the window of the *Warwick and Warwickshire Advertiser* to the effect that the war had effectively ended. Warwick went mad with joy. Travellers shouted and cheered from the trams. Church bells were rung and flags appeared everywhere. There were very mixed emotions, including many tears. The gun arrived in the Market Place, escorted by the mayor and aldermen, members of the fire brigade and numerous soldiers, many of whom had been wounded during the conflict. They were greeted by shouting, cheering and whistling.

The mayor then spoke about how 'the nightmare of the war had passed'. He added that there would be a proper celebration once the war had officially ended. Even as he spoke, numerous Chinese lanterns were released.

SCAPEGOAT SOLDIER SACKED

'**THERE IS NO** place for cowards like you in the British Army, and you will be cashiered dishonourably.'

For Lieutenant Colonel John Ford Elkington, the sentence of the court martial came as a terrible blow. It was also very unjust and unfair. Coming from a family of soldiers, John had served in various countries with the Royal Warwickshire Regiment. When war broke out in 1914, he was aged forty-nine and a lieutenant colonel in charge of the 1st Battalion. Whilst being killed by the enemy is one of the risks of being a soldier, John did not expect to have his career brutally terminated by his own side.

With Budbrooke Barracks, home to the Royal Warwickshire Regiment, situated just outside Warwick, John would have known the town well.

On 25 August 1914, the war was not going well for the British. This was the war which was popularly supposed to be over by Christmas – but nobody said which Christmas!

SCAPEGOATS

John and his men had been fighting for four days, without any respite. They had no food, were running short of ammunition, and had forgotten what sleep was. To make matters worse, they had no means of finding the rest of their brigade.

Originally they had gone to the aid of another regiment, and suffered heavy casualties in the process. John was left with no alternative but to retreat. Amongst the capable officers in his battalion was the young Bernard Law, later to become Viscount Montgomery of El Alamein.

John moved the remnants of his men back to nearby St Quentin, where he met a detachment of the Dublin Fusiliers who were in a similar state to his own troops. The soldiers were so exhausted that they slept standing up, and even whilst being fired upon. In an attempt to get some food from the local residents, Colonel Mainwaring, who was in charge of the Dubliners, approached the mayor with an interpreter.

The mayor, however, was more concerned for safety of his townspeople, knowing that many of them would be killed if a pitched battle took place in the town. Being a humane and practical man, John accepted his reasoning, and it was agreed that an attempt to halt the Germans would be made away from the residential area.

Only then did the mayor agree to provide food for the troops. But first John and Colonel Mainwaring had to sign an agreement to what they had arranged. Just after they had signed it, reinforcements arrived, and the written agreement no longer had any meaning.

In the ensuing confusion it was lost.

Unfortunately it was found by the Army hierarchy, who interpreted it as a written agreement to surrender to the enemy. At their subsequent court martial, John and Colonel Mainwaring were cleared of the charges of cowardice, but guilty of conspiring to surrender. Consequently they were dishonourably discharged from the Army.

Severely punishing any offender, regardless of rank, was one way that the military hierarchy adopted to disguise their own failings.

Mainwaring left the Army quietly, but not John. He had other ideas.

A few weeks later, he had joined the French Foreign Legion, and continued fighting the Germans. As an experienced soldier he was a great asset to the Legion, although he held no rank.

Life in the Legion was much tougher than in the Warwickshire Regiment, but John endured all the hardships. He always carried a copy of Rudyard Kipling's poem *If* with him wherever he went, and swore that it kept him going during the really difficult times.

He soon returned to the Front.

French Foreign Legion trooper in the desert. (Library of Congress, LC-DIG-ds-00728)

A year later he was severely wounded whilst leading a charge against a German stronghold. Although in agony for many hours, he continued directing his fellow legionnaires in their ultimately successful attack. In time he was awarded the Medaille Militaire and the Croix de Guerre by the French for his bravery.

During the next eight months he underwent several operations before being discharged from hospital, but his soldiering days were over.

ROYAL SUMMONS

Four days after returning to England, he received a summons which could not be ignored.

It had come from King George V at Buckingham Palace.

The king had heard of John's ill-treatment, and he was appalled at the injustice of the sentence. At a private investiture, he awarded John the Distinguished Service Order for his bravery in France.

But that was not all.

BERNARD LAW MONTGOMERY (1887-1976)

Monty, as he was normally known, joined the Royal Warwickshire Regiment as a second lieutenant in 1908. His military career progressed during the First and Second World Wars.

He escaped from Dunkirk, but really sprung to fame when he defeated Rommel at El Alamein in 1942, from where he fought up into Europe. His crowning moment was when he accepted the German surrender on Lüneburg Heath in 1945.

In time he was created 1st Viscount Montgomery of El Alamein, and his banner is laid up at St Mary's church in Warwick.

German prisoners captured and searched at El Alamein. (Library of Congress, LC-DIG-ds-01142)

He also gave him a pardon and reinstated him in his former rank of lieutenant colonel with all its privileges, which enabled him to wear his medals again with pride.

It was a big put down for the Army who had unreasonably and unfairly used him as a scapegoat to cover up their incompetence.

WARWICK AT WAR

I N SPITE OF being close to Coventry, and unlike neighbouring Kenilworth and Leamington, Warwick did not suffer too much from enemy action. Its Member of Parliament was Anthony Eden, who wanted peace but not appeasement. He resigned as Foreign Secretary in 1938, in protest against Neville Chamberlain's visit to Hitler. His actions were well supported by his constituents, and by Winston Churchill.

He was back in government soon after war broke out.

HOME FRONT

By 14 May 1940 Eden was the Secretary of State for War, at a time when things were not going well in the struggle against Hitler. The British Expeditionary Force was in retreat, and the future did not look very hopeful – and there was the very real possibility that the country would be invaded. With this in mind, Eden used the radio to broadcast his famous appeal to the country for men to form the Local Defence Volunteers. Soon afterwards, their name was changed to the Home Guard.

As the threat of air raids grew, shelters were built. One in Warwick was in the Pageant Gardens.

Wartime food controls led to the closure of some local slaughter houses. This resulted in animals from Warwick Market being taken to Coventry for slaughter and returned to Leamington for distribution: all at a time when there was petrol rationing!

FIRE WATCHING

St Mary's church tower is the highest place in Warwick, and it was used by members of the Special Constabulary and others for fire-watching duties. One morning, before the night shift went off duty, they reported having seen the glow of a large fire in the distance – they thought it could have been Northampton. It was actually London at the height of the Blitz: the flames could be seen a good 100 miles away.

The Luftwaffe used St Mary's as a marker when they headed for Coventry. On a particular night, as they flew overhead, the fire watchers could see a light apparently signalling to them from the vicinity of the Butts. At the end of their shift they reported what they had seen. When they went on duty the next night they were handed a special mounting device and a rifle: when they saw the signalling light again, they aimed the rifle at it, clamped it position and reported back. Police officers went into the tower and identified the house where the weapon was aimed, and a foreign woman was later arrested.

Sadly no official record appears to exist of this incident, and my informant is long since dead.

HOSPITAL

The outbreak of war enabled Warwick Hospital to throw off its old workhouse image and move forward, becoming a fully equipped medical facility. Almost overnight it moved from 200 to 500 beds, with extra wards being created in glorified huts (many of which survived until the late 1980s). Once it was realised that air raids on Coventry would happen, it was very necessary to have medical facilities available for the casualties. Injured service personnel and locals were also included. The hospital did not differentiate between friends or foes, and treated wounded enemy prisoners of war. Between 1941 and 1942 the hospital received visits from the Duchess of Gloucester and the Princess Royal in appreciation of its work.

In 1943, locally billeted Czech soldiers presented numerous wooden toys for the children at the hospital in gratitude for how they had been received in Warwick.

GESTAPO STATE

One of the most embarrassing incidents of the war in Warwick concerned the activities of the chief constable, Edward Richard Busk Kemble, known to all as Commander Kemble.

A man with a naval background, Kemble had fought at the Battle of Jutland and was predicted to go far in the Navy. However, he suffered badly from sea-sickness. To advance beyond his current rank would have meant serving in a small ship, which he felt he could not do. Consequently he resigned in 1928 and became the chief constable of the Warwickshire Constabulary, with headquarters in Warwick.

Right from the beginning of his new career, Kemble became known as a harsh disciplinarian. In this he was aided by his deputy, Superintendent Herbert Scarborough Whitlock Wake, who always wrote in green ink. Some say that Wake was the real 'power behind the throne', and that he manipulated Kemble. Just after he retired, in 1947, Wake's car was badly damaged – and dissatisfied policemen were suspected.

The discipline records for this period contain all manner of punishments issued by Kemble for what seem to be trivial matters today, such as not saluting when he passed. On one occasion a disciplined officer got his own back by sprinkling parsley seed all over Kemble's lawn, effectively ruining the chief's pride and joy. With the outbreak of war, Kemble evicted the resident superintendent at headquarters, and turned his accommodation into a war room. Here Kemble kept maps and records of the events of the war as they unfolded. He slept at headquarters and had to be informed, day or night, of any important changes in the war. At the same time he kept up his Draconian ways.

In 1942 an official complaint was made against him to the Home Office, alleging that he ran the constabulary 'like a Gestapo state'. The Home Office has no record of any enquiry. However, the media reported that the complaint was not upheld, but he was instructed to moderate his ways.

A troubled man, Kemble committed suicide in 1948.

AD 1940

MURDERED BY NAZIS

'**I**T IS CLEAR to me, however, that the commander is responsible for the actions and conduct of his regiment.'

With these words, SS-Obergruppenführer (equivalent to a lieutenant general) Josef 'Sepp' Dietrich, commander of the Leibstandarte SS, ensured that his name would be forever remembered in the annals of infamy.

In May 1940, the war against Nazi Germany was not going well: in fact, it was going exceptionally badly. So much for the experts who maintained that this was another war which would be over by Christmas! On 22 May, the 2nd Battalion of the Royal Warwickshire Regiment was fighting a rear-guard action, as the British Expeditionary Force retreated across Northern Europe. They were pursued by the unstoppable and victorious German troops.

HOLD TO THE LAST MAN

For the Warwickshires this was not just a retreat: along with other troops, they had been given the task of defending the outer ring of the retreat as the fleeing troops headed towards Dunkirk and, hopefully, embarkation back to England.

They had received specific instructions:

> Hold your present positions at all costs, to the last man and last round. This is essential that a vitally important operation may take place.

Dietrich (left) with Hitler and Himmler. (Bundesarchiv, Bild 183-C05557, CC-BY-SA-3.0, via Wikimedia Commons)

The operation was the evacuation of troops from Dunkirk.

Men given such an order knew their task could only end in death or captivity. As Germany was a party to the Geneva Convention, the men thought that, at the very least, prisoners could expect to be treated honourably. Tragically, the few survivors of the 2nd Battalion were to discover this was not to be the case.

In the following days, the Warwickshires gave a good account of themselves. They certainly delayed the German advance, and enabled more troops to escape. The Warwickshires had marched through the night of 25 May, and taken up a defensive position in and around Wormhout, in the Pas de Calais region of France. Although enjoying a welcome respite from enemy action, there was little or no rest for the defenders who now dug themselves in. It was a different story at Dunkirk, where a huge pall of smoke hung over the port following continuous attacks by the Luftwaffe.

By 27 May the weather had started to break, and the Warwickshires realised the extent of their task. Food and ammunition were in short supply, and so were maps of the area. In particular, there was a noticeable lack of vital anti-tank weapons. Their flagging morale was not helped by the steady flow of retreating troops, all heading for Dunkirk and home. Matters were then made worse by a heavy air raid on Wormhout.

NAZI ATROCITY

On the ground, the advancing Germans were not finding it easy. They were encountering stiff resistance, and taking casualties. It was during this advance that Josef Dietrich was posted as missing. His disappearance did not endear the defending troops to their attackers, and may have led to what occurred when the defenders surrendered. Dietrich reappeared several hours later, having been forced to shelter in a ditch for several hours.

On 28 May the defenders, a mixture of officers and other ranks from the Warwickshires, the Cheshires and the Royal Artillery, were overrun. Believing that they would be treated fairly as prisoners of war, they surrendered. These beliefs were quickly shattered by their captors. The SS had taken many casualties, and were in no mood to be generous. In fact, they wanted revenge – and these captured troops would do very nicely. The prisoners were moved

WIFE'S BELIEF

Mrs Kathleen West, wife of Royal Warwickshire Private Reginald West, who escaped from Wormhout, never lost hope that he would survive the war and come home. She refused to believe the letter from the War Office advising her that he was missing: presumed dead. In the end she was proved right, and he returned.

JOHN ENOCH POWELL (1912-1998)

In 1939 Enoch, as he was usually called, had been a professor in Ancient Greek at Sydney University. By October he had returned to England and enlisted as a private soldier in the Royal Warwickshire Regiment. He was quickly promoted and transferred to Military Intelligence, and later to other staff positions. Much to his chagrin, Enoch never saw active service (although this may have saved his life). When the war ended, he held the rank of brigadier in the Warwickshires. It was whilst he was a government minister that he made his well-remembered speech on the dangers of immigration, in which he warned of rivers of blood. For Enoch, it was effectively the end of his political career.

Enoch always had a love for Warwick, and regularly attended regimental re-unions. He is buried in Warwick Cemetery, and there is a memorial plaque to him in the Regimental Chapel at St Mary's church.

---

away, in double time, for the best part of a mile. Any wounded men who could not keep up were shot or bayoneted. Other prisoners were made to hold their hands in the air for more than fifteen minutes. Finally, the men were herded into a barn.

And the massacre began.

The first few prisoners were taken out of the barn in groups of five and shot. When the German troops decided that this method was taking too long, they threw hand-grenades into the barn, and sprayed the men with automatic fire.

SURVIVORS

Contrary to what the Nazis intended, there were a few survivors. Some men had forced their way out of the rear of the barn, and others managed to shelter underneath the bodies of their comrades. Those who were later captured by members of the German Wehrmacht, generally a far more honourable institution, were properly treated.

With peace in May 1945, this massacre was one of several similar incidents investigated by the victorious Allies. Problems began straightaway, mainly owing to the lack of witnesses.

In their over-enthusiastic quest for convictions, some of the Allied investigators employed tactics which were similar to those used by the men they were investigating. When this torture was revealed it had a serious effect on the outcome of several trials. Dietrich was sentenced to twenty-five years' imprisonment for the murder of ninety American prisoners just outside Malmedy (an easier case to prove). However, because of the way he had been interrogated he was released after serving just ten years. He was then sentenced to a further eighteen months of imprisonment for pre-war Nazi crimes, and died soon after his release.

FURTHER READING AND ACKNOWLEDGEMENTS

A History of Warwick and its People by Thomas Kemp
Assorted internet and magazine articles
Captain Swing by Eric Hobsbawm and George Rudé
Chartism by Harry Browne
Curious Clerics by Graham Sutherland
Daisy: The Life and Loves of the Countess of Warwick by Sushila Anand
Dastardly Deeds in Victorian Warwickshire by Graham Sutherland
Guy's Cliffe: Back to its Roots by Bob Dixon
Hamlyn History of Torture
Leamington Lives Remembered by Alan Griffin
Massacre on the Road to Dunkirk by Leslie Aitken
Midland History Journal
More Ripples from Warwickshire's Past by Paul Bolitho
My Darling Daisy by Theo Lang
Mysteries of Police and Crime by Major Arthur Griffiths
Olive Princess of Cumberland (1772 – 1834) by Miles Macnair
One Morning in May by Patrick Heyes
Richard Beauchamp Medieval England's Greatest Knight by David Brindley
Ripples from Warwickshire's Past by Paul Bolitho
Terrible Murder of a Policeman by Joseph Poland
The Black Book of Warwick by Thomas Kemp
The Chronicle
The Common Hangman by James Bland
The Gunpowder Plot: Terror and Faith in 1605 by Antonia Fraser
The Leamington and Warwick Tramways by S.L. Swingle and K. Turner
The Past in Warwick: Tudors to Victorians edited by Nat Alcock
The Town and Castle of Warwick by William Field
The Warwick Recorder
The Warwickshire Soldier by *Evening Telegraph*
Tolpuddle Martyrs by Trades Union Congress
Warwick and Warwickshire Advertiser
Warwick (The Kingmaker) by C W Oman
Warwick Court Leet Archives
Warwick in Times Past by PJE Gates
Warwick's Most Famous Son: The Story of Thomas Oken and his Charity by Paul Bolitho
Warwickshire Crimes and Criminals by Graham Sutherland
Warwickshire Constabulary Archives
You We Salute compiled by Roy Rowberry

The late Roger Higgins
The late Ray Tisdale
The late John Thornton
Other Warwick residents who shared memories with me, but which were not used in this publication